The Basic Oxford Picture Dictionary

Margot F. Gramer

Illustrations by:

Skip Baker
Graphic Chart & Map Co.
Karen Loccisano
Laura Hartman Maestro
M. Chandler Martylewski
Yoshi Miyake
Joel Snyder

Oxford University Press

Oxford University Press

200 Madison Avenue
New York, NY 10016 USA

Walton Street
Oxford OX2 6DP England

OXFORD and OXFORD AMERICAN ENGLISH are trademarks of
Oxford University Press.

Library of Congress Cataloging-in-Publication Data

Gramer, Margot.
    The basic Oxford picture dictionary / Margot Gramer.
        p. cm.
    ISBN 0-19-434468-1
    1. Picture dictionaries, English. I. Title.
PE1629.G68 1993   92-35497
423'.1—dc20   CIP

ISBN 0-19-434468-1

Illustrations by: Skip Baker, Karen Loccisano, Laura Hartman
Maestro, M. Chandler Martylewski, Yoshi Miyake, Joel Snyder,
Graphic Chart & Map Co.

Icons by Stephan Van Litsenborg

Editorial Manager: Susan Lanzano
Editors: Paul Phillips, Jeffrey Krum
Designers: Mark C. Kellogg, Alan Barnett
Art Buyer/Researcher: Karen Polyak
Production Manager: Abram Hall

Cover Design: Mark C. Kellogg
Cover Illustration: Karen Loccisano

Printing (last digit): 10 9 8 7 6 5 4 3 2

Printed in Hong Kong

The Basic Oxford Picture Dictionary has been developed to meet the needs of low-beginning level adult and young adult ESL students and is an ideal resource for students with limited literacy skills.

The Basic Oxford Picture Dictionary illustrates some 1,200 words and phrases most relevant to the everyday experience of adult and young adult learners. Vocabulary is presented in beautiful full-color illustrations which depict each entry in its real-life context. Pages may be used at random, depending on the students' particular needs. The book need not be taught in order. Together with its components, the Dictionary forms a comprehensive and flexible program for the teaching of key, everyday vocabulary and basic survival skills.

The words depicted are those most useful for students needing basic English skills. The most common name for any given item is used for simplicity. When two common names for an item exist, both are often included.

The Basic Oxford Picture Dictionary contextualizes vocabulary whenever possible, thus making the language learner's task easier. Nouns, adjectives, and prepositions are identified by number; verbs are identified by letter.

Larger, easier-to-read type and a limited number of words per page help make the Dictionary more accessible to low-beginning level learners. In addition, illustrations are consecutively numbered, left to right, top to bottom, wherever possible.

An index and pronunciation guide in the Appendix help students and teachers locate words and their correct pronunciation quickly. A complete set of Dictionary Cassettes offers a reading of all of the words in the Dictionary.

Other components available for use with The Basic Oxford Picture Dictionary are: The Teacher's Resource Book and Cassette, the Workbook, Picture Cards, Wall Charts, and Overhead Transparencies for each illustrated Dictionary page.

CONTENTS

		Page
1. **Everyday Language**		**2-10**
	An ESL Classroom	2
	Time: Months and Seasons	4
	Time: A Calendar	5
	Time: Times of Day	6
	Time: The Clock	7
	Weather	8
	Shapes and Colors	9
	Money	10
2. **People**		**11-15**
	People	11
	Describing People	12
	Daily Routines	14
3. **Family**		**16-21**
	Family	16
	A Birthday Party	17
	Feelings	18
	Life Events	20
4. **The Home**		**22-33**
	Houses and Surroundings	22
	An Apartment Building	23
	A Living Room	24
	A Kitchen	25
	A Bedroom	26
	A Bathroom	27
	Housework	28
	Cleaning Implements	30
	Tools for the Home	31
	Household Problems	32

5. The Market $34-41$

Vegetables	34
Fruits	35
Meat and Seafood	36
Packaging	37
Dairy Products and Other Foods	38
Shopping at the Supermarket	40

6. Meal Time $42-47$

A Table Setting	42
At a Restaurant	43
Common Prepared Foods	44
Cooking a Meal	46

7. Clothes $48-57$

Basic Clothes	48
Casual Clothes	49
Cold Weather Clothes	50
Underwear and Sleepwear	51
Describing Clothes	52
At the Store (Prepositions I)	54
Jewelry and Accessories	55
Taking Care of Clothes: The Laundromat	56
Taking Care of Clothes: The Tailor / Dry Cleaner	57

8. Health $58-67$

The Body	58
The Face and Head	60
Toiletries	61
Aches, Pains, and Injuries	62
Treatments	64
First Aid and Health Care Items	65
At a Medical Office	66

9. The Community 68–75

The Community 68
Banking 70
The Post Office 71
An Intersection 72
Emergencies and Natural Disasters 74

10. Transportation 76–81

Transportation 76
Parts of a Car 77
On the Road (Prepositions II) 78
At an Airport 80

11. Work 82–91

Occupations and Workplaces I 82
Occupations II 84
Occupations III 86
A Construction Site 87
At Work 88
A Day-Care Center 90

12. Recreation 92–95

Leisure 92
Celebrate the Holidays 94

Appendix 96

A. Maps 96
B. Numbers 100
C. Weights and Measures 101
D. Temperature Conversion 102

Index 103

1. (chalk)board
2. chalk
3. eraser
4. teacher
5. student
6. chair
7. desk
8. book
9. paper
10. pen
11. pencil
12. notebook
13. computer

A. write
B. point (to)
C. go out
D. come in
E. read
F. listen
G. work at the computer

H. look at the screen
I. close the window
J. open a notebook
K. raise…hand
L. talk
M. sit
N. stand

① January
S	M	T	W	T	F	S
					1	2
3	4	5	6	7	8	9
10	11	12	13	14	15	16
17	18	19	20	21	22	23
24 31	25	26	27	28	29	30

(⑬)

② February
S	M	T	W	T	F	S
1	2	3	4	5	6	
7	8	9	10	11	12	13
14	15	16	17	18	19	20
21	22	23	24	25	26	27
28						

③ March
S	M	T	W	T	F	S
	1	2	3	4	5	6
7	8	9	10	11	12	13
14	15	16	17	18	19	20
21	22	23	24	25	26	27
28	29	30	31			

(⑭)

④ April
S	M	T	W	T	F	S
				1	2	3
4	5	6	7	8	9	10
11	12	13	14	15	16	17
18	19	20	21	22	23	24
25	26	27	28	29	30	

⑤ May
S	M	T	W	T	F	S
						1
2	3	4	5	6	7	8
9	10	11	12	13	14	15
16	17	18	19	20	21	22
23 30	24 31	25	26	27	28	29

⑥ June
S	M	T	W	T	F	S
	1	2	3	4	5	
6	7	8	9	10	11	12
13	14	15	16	17	18	19
20	21	22	23	24	25	26
27	28	29	30			

(⑮)

⑦ July
S	M	T	W	T	F	S
				1	2	3
4	5	6	7	8	9	10
11	12	13	14	15	16	17
18	19	20	21	22	23	24
25	26	27	28	29	30	31

⑧ August
S	M	T	W	T	F	S
1	2	3	4	5	6	7
8	9	10	11	12	13	14
15	16	17	18	19	20	21
22	23	24	25	26	27	28
29	30	31				

⑨ September
S	M	T	W	T	F	S
			1	2	3	4
5	6	7	8	9	10	11
12	13	14	15	16	17	18
19	20	21	22	23	24	25
26	27	28	29	30		

(⑯)

⑩ October
S	M	T	W	T	F	S
					1	2
3	4	5	6	7	8	9
10	11	12	13	14	15	16
17 24	18	19	20	21	22	23
31	25	26	27	28	29	30

⑪ November
S	M	T	W	T	F	S
	1	2	3	4	5	6
7	8	9	10	11	12	13
14	15	16	17	18	19	20
21	22	23	24	25	26	27
28	29	30				

⑫ December
S	M	T	W	T	F	S
			1	2	3	4
5	6	7	8	9	10	11
12	13	14	15	16	17	18
19	20	21	22	23	24	25
26	27	28	29	30	31	

1. January
2. February
3. March
4. April
5. May
6. June
7. July
8. August
9. September
10. October
11. November
12. December
13. winter
14. spring
15. summer
16. fall

January

① Sun.	② Mon.	③ Tues.	④ Wed.	⑤ Thurs.	⑥ Fri.	⑦ Sat.
					⑧ **1**	⑨ **2**
⑩ **3**	**4**	⑪ **5**	⑫ **(6)**	⑬ **7**	**8**	**9**
10	**11**	**12**	**13**	**14**	⑭ **15**	**16**
17	**18**	**19**	⑮ **20**	**21**	**22**	**23**
24 / **31**	**25**	**26**	**27**	**28**	**29**	**30**

⑯

JANUARY	FEBRUARY	MARCH	APRIL	MAY	JUNE	JULY	AUGUST	SEPTEMBER	OCTOBER	NOVEMBER	DECEMBER

1. Sunday	**9.** 2nd
2. Monday	**10.** 3rd
3. Tuesday	**11.** yesterday
4. Wednesday	**12.** today
5. Thursday	**13.** tomorrow
6. Friday	**14.** day
7. Saturday	**15.** week
8. 1st	**16.** year

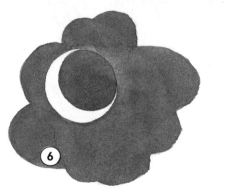

1. morning
2. afternoon
3. evening
4. night

5. sun
6. moon
7. stars

1. clock	**5.** ten fifteen
2. noon	**6.** ten thirty
3. midnight	**7.** ten forty-five
4. ten o'clock	

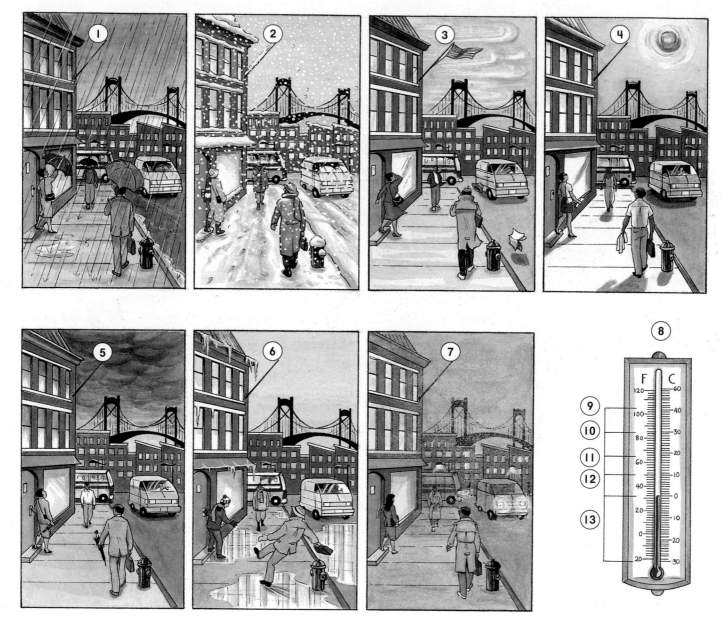

1. raining
2 snowing
3. windy
4. sunny
5. cloudy
6. icy
7. foggy

8. temperature
9. hot
10. warm
11. cool
12. cold
13. freezing

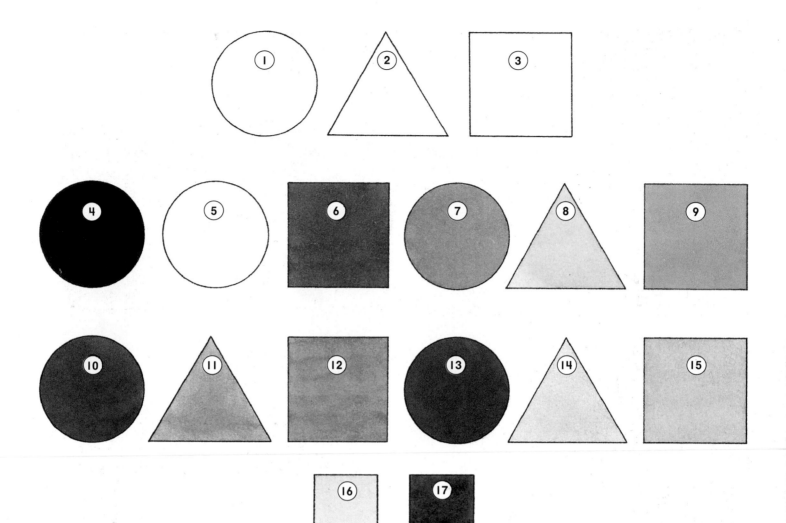

1. circle
2. triangle
3. square
4. black
5. white
6. red
7. blue
8. yellow
9. green

10. brown
11. gray
12. orange
13. purple
14. beige
15. pink
16. light (blue)
17. dark (blue)

1. bills
2. dollar
3. coins
4. penny
5. nickel
6. dime
7. quarter
8. cents
9. check
10. bill
11. receipt
12. credit card

1. baby
2. girl
3. boy
4. woman
5. man
6. child
7. teenager
8. adult

Height
1. tall
2. average height
3. short

Weight
4. heavy / fat
5. average weight
6. thin / skinny

Size
7. big / large
8. small / little

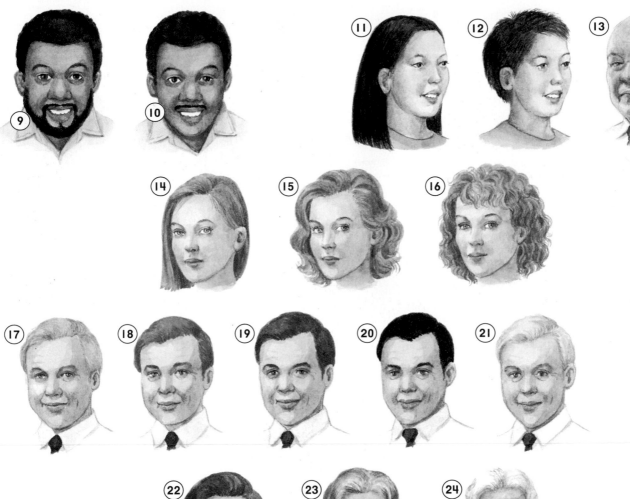

Hair

9. beard
10. mustache
11. long hair
12. short hair
13. bald
14. straight hair
15. wavy hair
16. curly hair

17. blond hair
18. red hair
19. brown hair
20. black hair
21. gray hair

Age

22. young
23. middle-aged
24. old

13

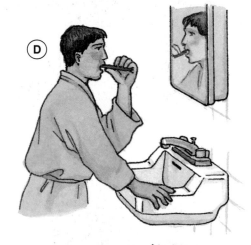

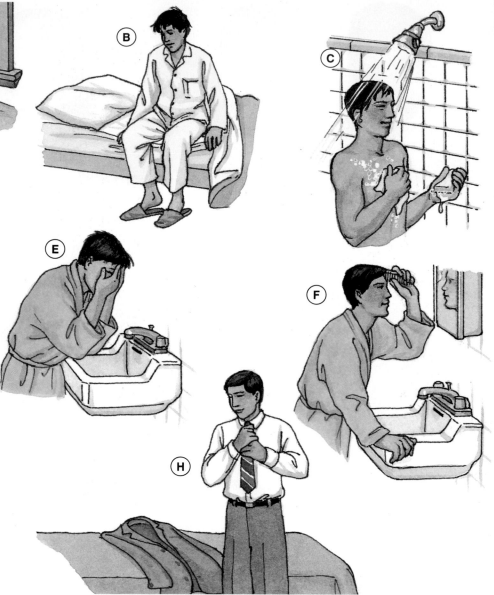

A. wake up

B. get up

C. take a shower

D. brush...teeth

tooth

E. wash...face

F. comb...hair

G. shave

H. get dressed

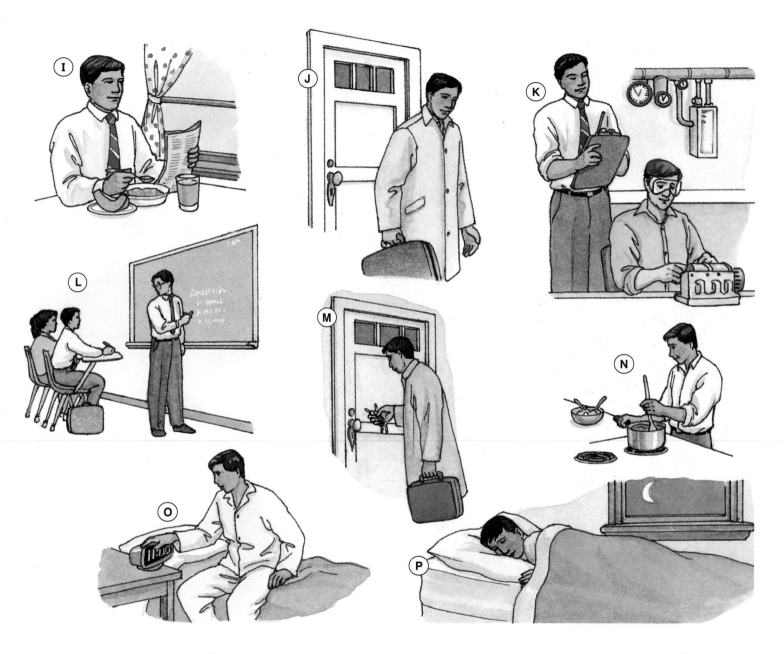

I. eat breakfast
J. leave the house
K. work
L. study/learn

M. come home
N. cook dinner
O. go to bed
P. go to sleep

1. grandparents
2. father
3. mother
4. sister
5. brother
6. uncle
7. aunt
8. cousins

9. husband
10. wife
11. parents
12. son
13. daughter
14. niece
15. nephew

A. give a present to
B. laugh
C. kiss
D. smile
E. sing

F. blow out the candles
G. take a picture
H. drink milk
I. cut the cake
J. open a card

1. angry
2. happy
3. sad
4. nervous

5. bored
6. scared
7. excited

8. surprised
9. worried
10. tired
11. hungry

12. thirsty
13. embarrassed
14. homesick

A. be born

B. start school

C. graduate

D. get a job

E. retire

F. fall in love
G. get married
H. get divorced
I. have a baby

J. move
K. get sick
L. die

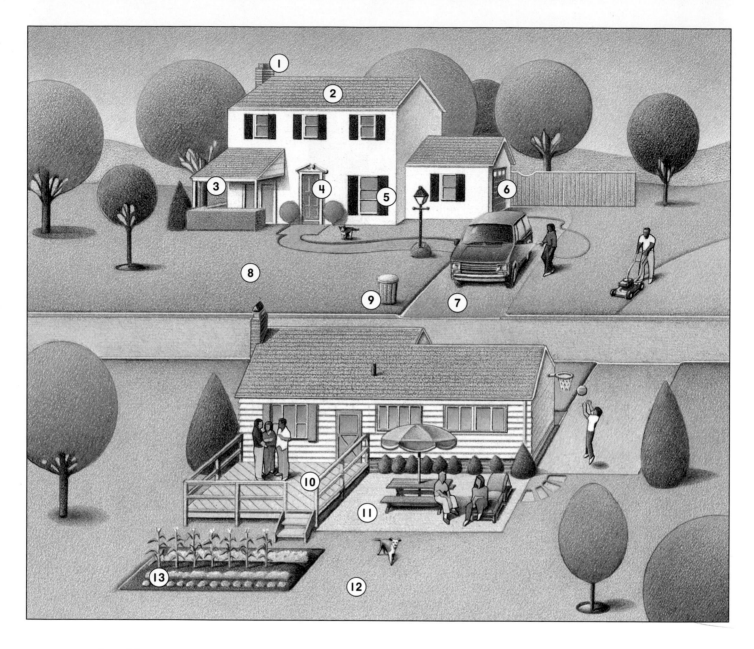

1. chimney	8. lawn
2. roof	9. garbage can
3. porch	10. deck
4. front door	11. patio
5. window	12. backyard
6. garage	13. garden
7. driveway	

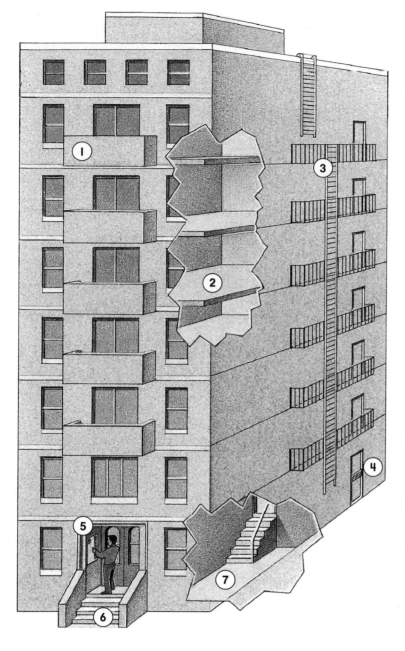

1. balcony
2. floor
3. fire escape
4. (fire) exit
5. entrance
6. steps
7. basement

8. hall
9. lobby
10. elevator
11. mailboxes
12. stairway / stairs
13. intercom

1. ceiling	**8.** end table
2. wall	**9.** coffee table
3. floor	**10.** rug
4. drapes	**11.** couch/sofa
5. armchair/easy chair	**12.** bookcase
6. lamp	**13.** stereo (system)
7. (tele)phone	**14.** television/TV

1. microwave (oven)
2. pot
3. (tea)kettle
4. burner
5. skillet/(frying) pan
6. stove/range
7. oven
8. broiler
9. can opener
10. kitchen sink
11. trash can
12. cabinet
13. toaster
14. counter
15. freezer
16. refrigerator

1. closet
2. dresser/bureau
3. drawer
4. air conditioner
5. curtains
6. carpet
7. bed

8. pillow
9. pillowcase
10. bedspread
11. blanket
12. sheets
13. alarm clock
14. night table

1. shower
2. shower curtain
3. faucet
4. drain
5. bathtub
6. wastebasket
7. sink

8. mirror
9. medicine chest/
   medicine cabinet
10. hamper
11. towel
12. toilet
13. toilet paper

A. make the bed

B. pick up/straighten up
the room

C. clean the bathroom

D. vacuum the rug

E. dust the furniture

F. wash the dishes

G. dry the dishes

H. water the plants

I. rake the leaves

J. take out the garbage

K. empty the wastebasket

L. change the sheets

M. sweep the floor

N. wash the windows

O. mop the floor

P. do the laundry

Q. plant a tree

R. mow the lawn

1. mop
2. broom
3. dustpan
4. vacuum cleaner
5. cloth/rag
6. cleanser

7. rubber gloves
8. (scrub) brush
9. sponge
10. paper towels
11. bucket
12. outlet

1. pliers
2. wrench
3. screwdriver
4. hammer
5. saw
6. drill
7. tape measure
8. flashlight

9. toolbox
10. (step)ladder
11. hose
12. rake
13. shovel
14. lawn mower
15. nail
16. screw

1. leaking roof / ceiling
2. cracked wall
3. broken window
4. cracked ceiling
5. no heat
6. stopped-up toilet
7. no hot water
8. broken lock

9. broken steps
10. dripping faucet
11. clogged drain
12. refrigerator not working

13. (cock)roaches
14. mice
15. flooded basement

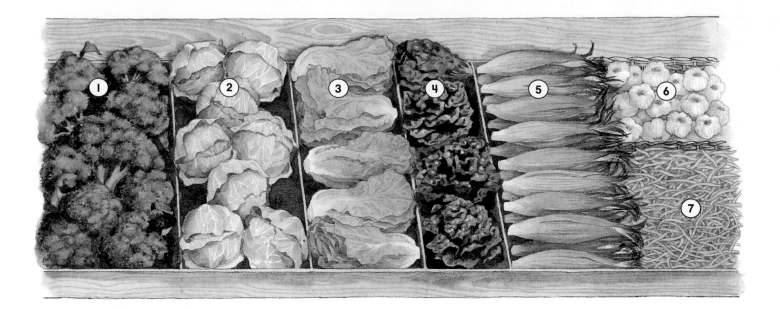

1. broccoli
2. cabbage
3. lettuce
4. spinach
5. corn
6. garlic
7. string beans
8. tomato

9. (bell) pepper
10. cucumber
11. potato
12. onion
13. carrot
14. mushrooms
15. peas

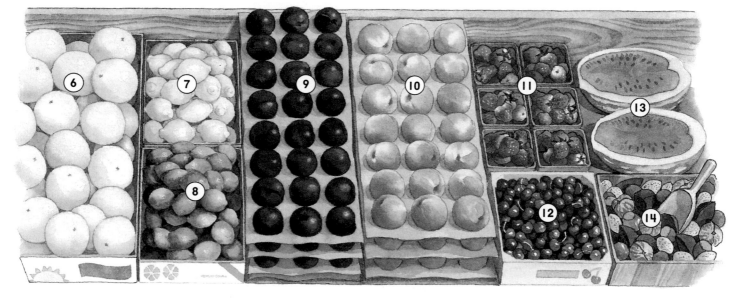

1. bananas
2. grapes
3. apples
4. oranges
5. pears
6. grapefruit
7. lemons

8. limes
9. plums
10. peaches
11. strawberries
12. cherries
13. watermelons
14. nuts

1. beef
2. steak
3. ground meat
4. pork
5. bacon
6. ham
7. lamb
8. chicken
9. turkey
10. fish
11. lobster
12. shrimp
13. clams

1. a carton of milk
2. a container of yogurt
3. a bottle of soda
4. a package of cookies
5. a loaf of bread
6. a bag of flour
7. a jar of coffee
8. a can of soup
9. a roll of toilet paper
10. a box of cereal
11. a bar of soap
12. a tube of toothpaste

1. milk
2. cream
3. sugar
4. eggs
5. cheese
6. butter
7. margarine

8. yogurt
9. bread
10. cereal
11. coffee
12. tea
13. flour
14. oil

15. rice
16. (dried) beans
17. pasta/noodles
18. soup
19. soda/pop
20. juice

21. cookies
22. salt
23. pepper
24. mustard
25. ketchup
26. mayonnaise

1. shelf
2. aisle
3. shopping basket
4. shopping cart
5. customer
6. checker / checkout person
7. scale
8. cash register
9. checkout (counter)
10. groceries
11. bag
12. packer / bagger
13. bottle return

A. push	**E.** put in
B. carry	**F.** take out
C. pay for	**G.** weigh
D. choose / pick out	**H.** pack

1. table
2. silverware
3. place mat
4. bowl
5. plate
6. glass
7. cup

8. saucer
9. salt and pepper shakers
10. napkin
11. fork
12. knife
13. spoon

1. cook
2. dishwasher
3. booth
4. water
5. busboy
6. waiter
7. waitress
8. menu
9. high chair
10. smoking section
11. no smoking section
12. cashier

Breakfast

Lunch OR

1. scrambled eggs
2. sausage
3. fried eggs
4. toast
5. muffin/English muffin
6. waffles
7. pancakes

8. syrup
9. donuts
10. sandwich
11. hamburger
12. french fries
13. hot dog

Dinner

Dessert

14. salad
15. spaghetti
16. pizza
17. baked potato
18. pork chop

19. mashed potatoes
20. fried chicken
21. ice cream
22. apple pie

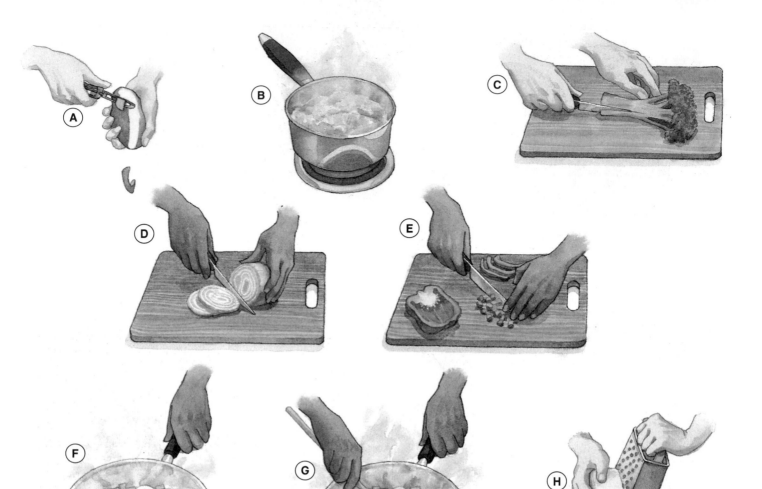

A. peel potatoes
B. boil water
C. cut broccoli
D. slice onions

E. chop peppers
F. fry onions and peppers
G. stir onions and peppers
H. grate cheese

I. steam vegetables

J. pour milk

K. mix ingredients

L. bake a casserole

M. broil fish

1. dress
2. blouse
3. skirt
4. shirt
5. tie
6. belt
7. pants
8. shoe
9. suit
10. cap
11. uniform

1. swimtrunks / bathing suit
2. swimsuit / bathing suit
3. sunglasses
4. jeans
5. sandals

6. baseball cap
7. T-shirt
8. sneakers / athletic shoes
9. shorts
10. warm-up suit

1. jacket
2. (down) vest
3. sweater
4. hat
5. sweatshirt
6. backpack
7. boots
8. raincoat
9. umbrella
10. scarf
11. coat
12. mittens
13. gloves
14. earmuffs

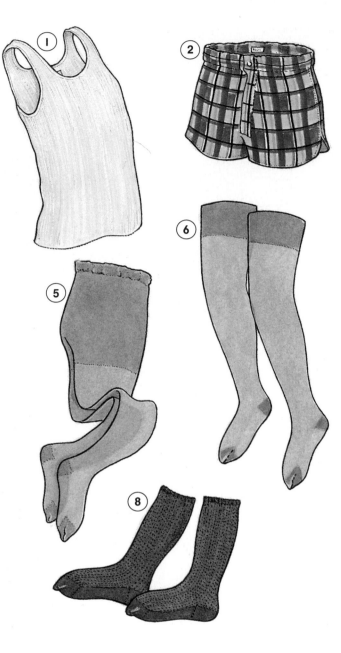

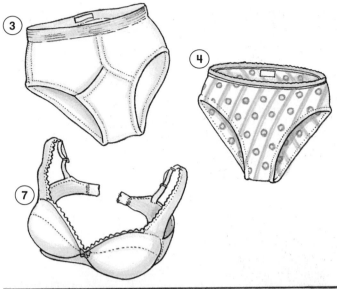

1. undershirt
2. boxer shorts
3. underpants
4. panties
5. pantyhose
6. stockings

7. bra
8. socks
9. nightgown
10. pajamas
11. bathrobe
12. slippers

1. heavy
2. light
3. new
4. old
5. clean

6. dirty
7. high
8. low
9. narrow
10. wide

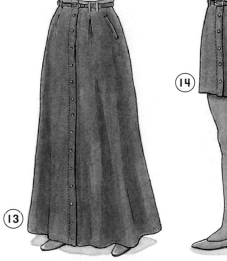

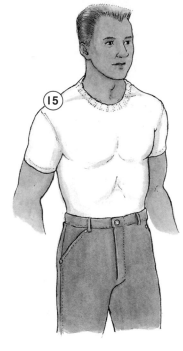

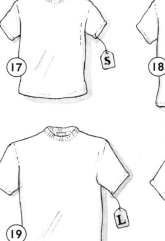

11. wet
12. dry
13. long
14. short
15. tight

16. loose
17. small
18. medium
19. large
20. extra-large

53

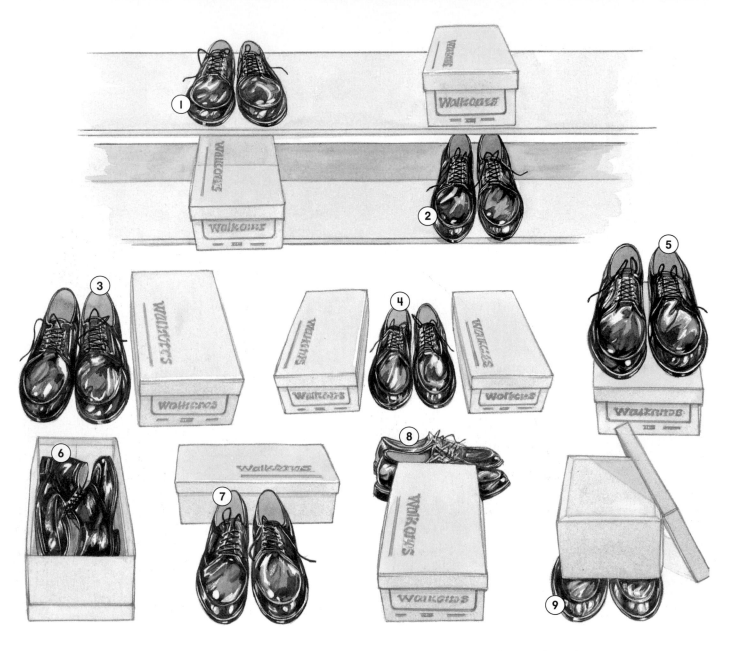

1. above the box
2. below the box
3. next to the box
4. between the boxes
5. on the box
6. in the box
7. in front of the box
8. behind the box
9. under the box

1. ring
2. bracelet
3. earrings
4. necklace
5. purse/bag

6. watch
7. change
8. glasses
9. wallet
10. ID card

1. washer / washing machine
2. detergent
3. dryer
4. slot
5. laundry basket
6. ironing board
7. iron

A. load / put in
B. unload / take out
C. iron
D. fold

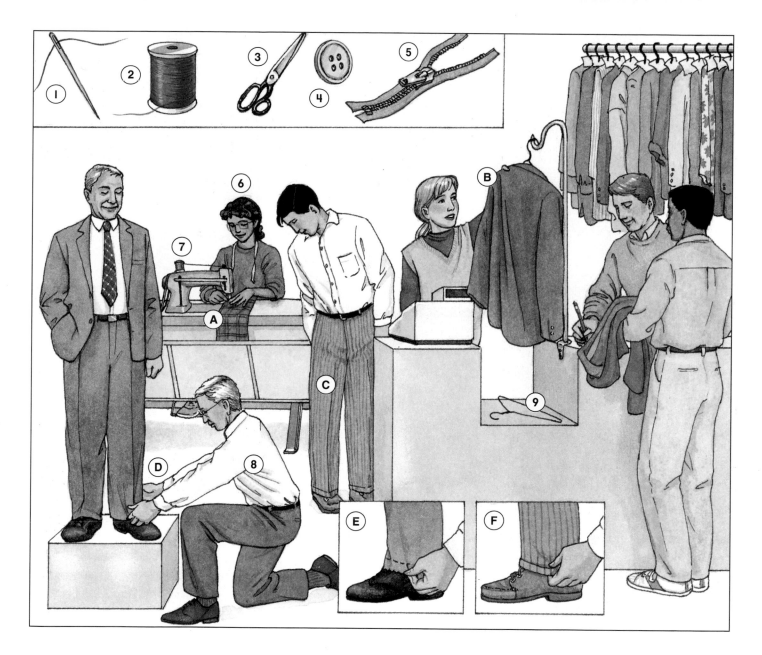

1. needle
2. thread
3. scissors
4. button
5. zipper
6. seamstress
7. sewing machine
8. tailor
9. hanger

A. sew
B. hang up
C. try on
D. alter/do alterations
E. lengthen
F. shorten

1. face
2. neck
3. shoulder
4. chest
5. hand
6. waist
7. hip

8. finger
9. thumb
10. wrist
11. head
12. arm
13. breast
14. leg

15. back
16. thigh
17. elbow
18. knee
19. calf
20. ankle
21. foot

22. heel
23. toe
24. brain
25. lung
26. heart
27. stomach

59

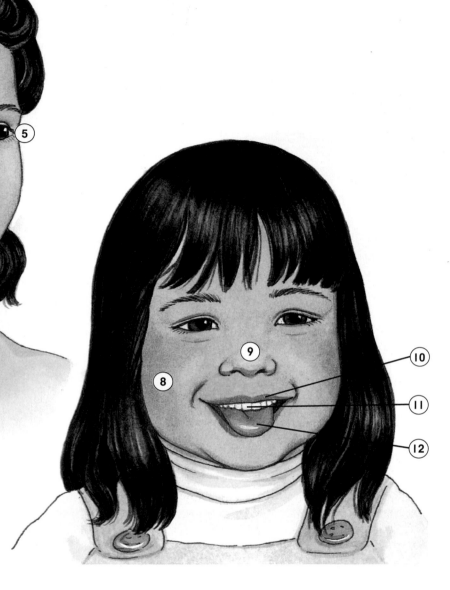

1. hair
2. forehead
3. ear
4. eyebrow
5. eye
6. mouth

7. chin
8. cheek
9. nose
10. lip
11. tooth
12. tongue

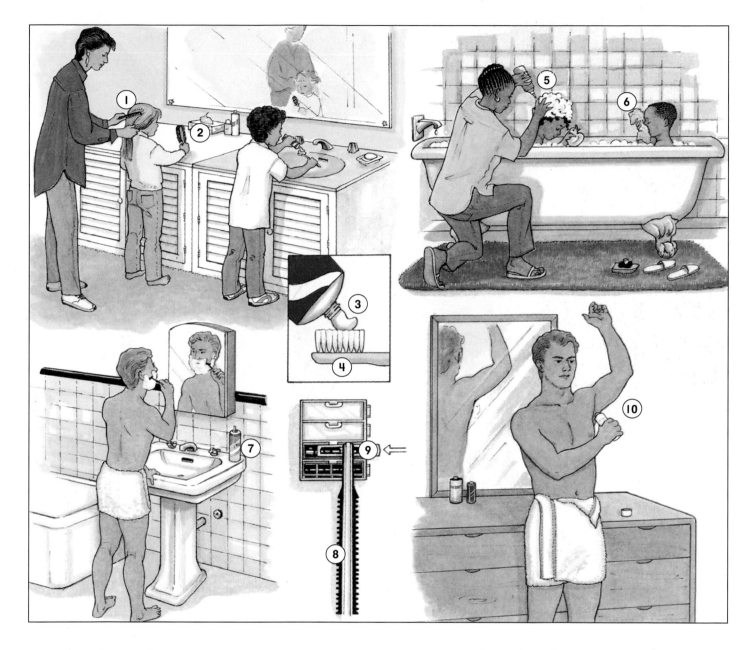

1. comb
2. brush
3. toothpaste
4. toothbrush
5. shampoo

6. washcloth
7. shaving cream
8. razor
9. blades
10. deodorant

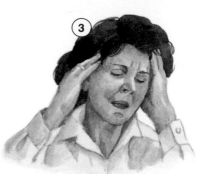
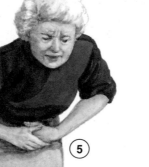
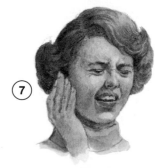
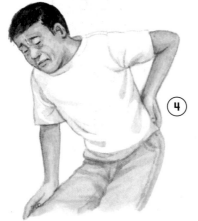
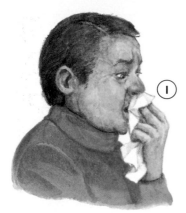
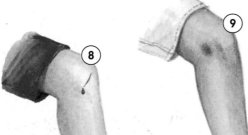

1. cold
2. fever
3. headache
4. backache
5. stomachache
6. toothache

7. earache
8. cut
9. bruise
10. rash
11. insect bite
12. sore throat

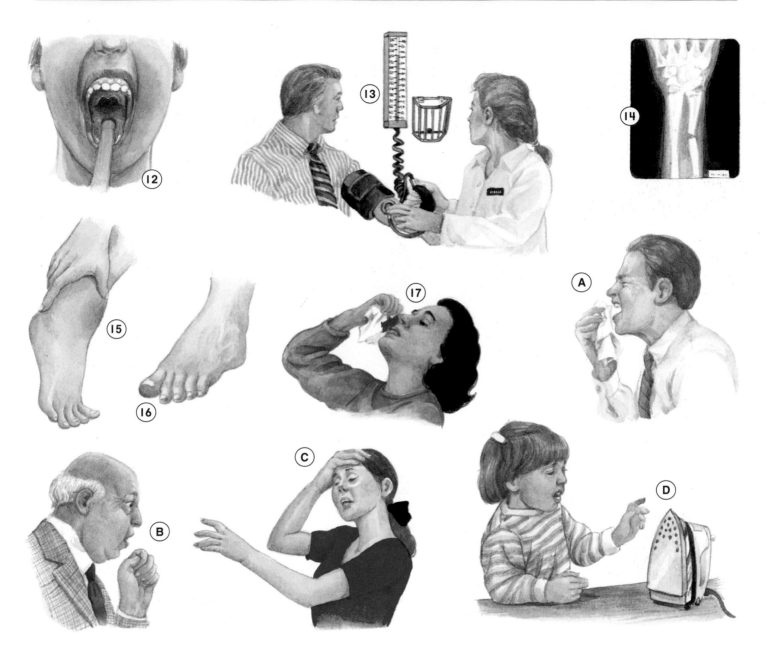

13. high blood pressure
14. broken arm
15. swollen ankle
16. infected toe
17. bloody nose

A. sneeze
B. cough
C. faint
D. burn...self

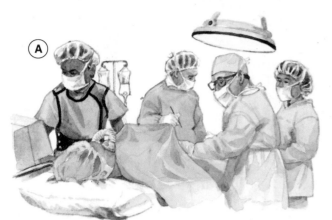

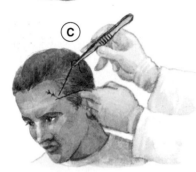

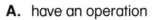

A. have an operation

B. get rest

C. get stitches

D. take medicine

E. get a cast

F. exercise

G. go on a diet

1. medicine / drugs

2. pills

3. cream / ointment

4. injection / shot

5. drops

6. medicine dropper

7. spray

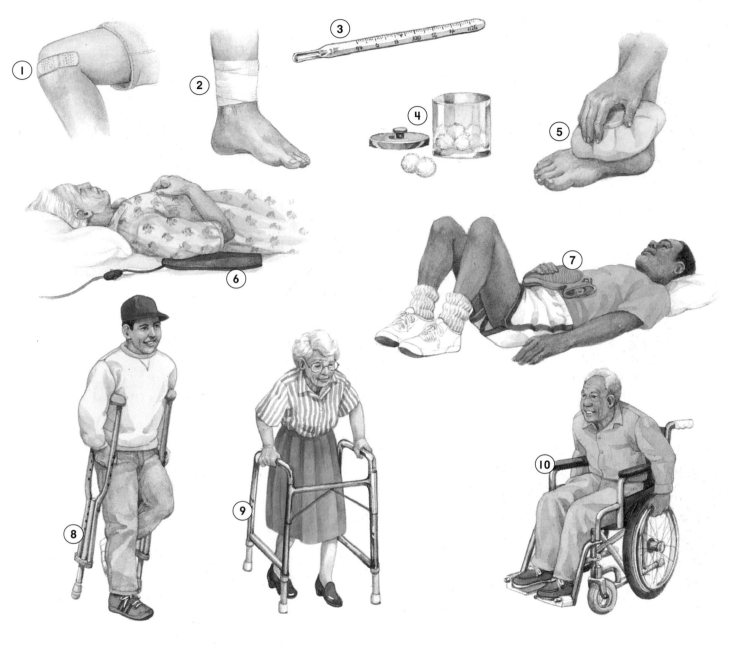

1. Band-Aid
2. bandage
3. thermometer
4. cotton balls
5. ice pack

6. heating pad
7. hot water bottle
8. crutches
9. walker
10. wheelchair

1. waiting room
2. receptionist
3. insurance form
4. insurance card
5. patient

6. doctor
7. nurse
8. examining room
9. X ray
10. prescription

A. fill out the form
B. print name
C. sign name
D. show insurance card
E. wait

F. examine the patient
G. weigh the patient
H. take…temperature
I. give a shot / an injection
J. write a prescription

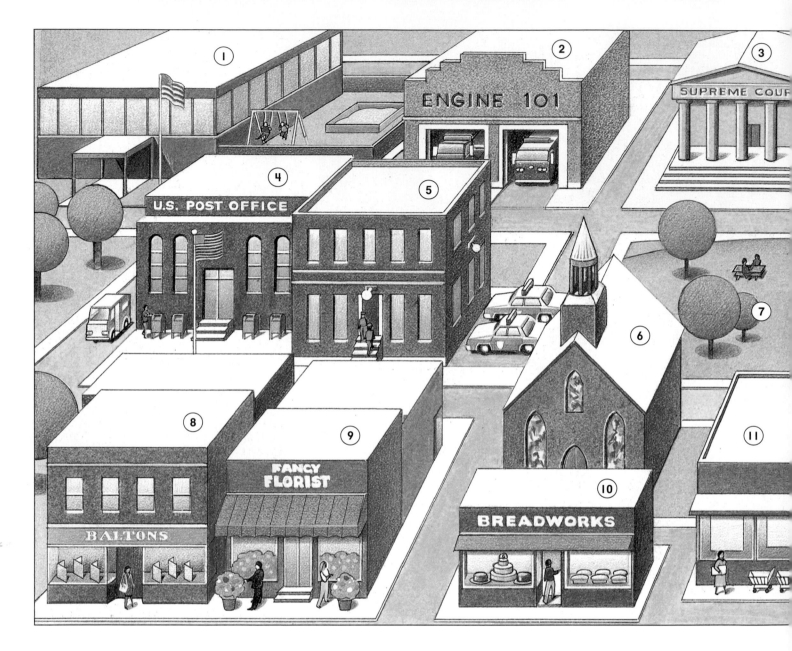

1. school
2. firehouse
3. courthouse
4. post office
5. police station

6. church
7. park
8. bookstore
9. florist
10. bakery
11. supermarket

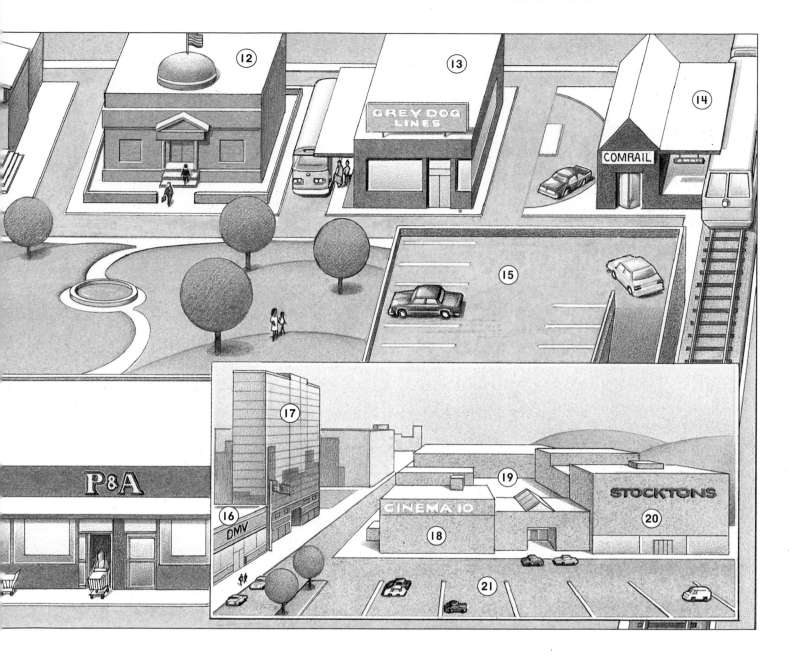

12. city hall
13. bus station
14. train station
15. parking garage
16. Department of Motor
    Vehicles (DMV)

17. office building
18. movie theater
19. mall
20. department store
21. parking lot

1. teller
2. drive-thru window
3. security guard
4. ATM/cash machine
5. line
6. check
7. date
8. amount
9. signature
10. withdrawal slip
11. deposit slip

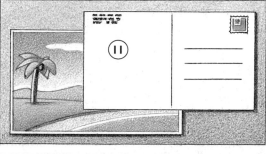

1. postal worker /
   postal clerk
2. package
3. letter carrier
4. mailbox
5. letter
6. envelope

7. return address
8. stamp
9. address
10. zip code
11. postcard
12. money order

1. traffic light
2. pedestrian
3. crosswalk
4. public telephone
5. corner
6. intersection
7. newsstand
8. parking meter
9. sidewalk
10. curb
11. bus stop
12. bench

A. come out of the store	**G.** buy groceries
B. go into the store	**H.** look at the windows/clothes
C. make a phone call	
D. stop	**I.** walk
E. cross the street	**J.** turn
F. mail a letter	**K.** wait for the bus

1. smoke
2. fire
3. fire fighter
4. accident
5. ambulance
6. paramedic
7. robbery / theft
8. police officer
9. mugging
10. flood
11. earthquake
12. tornado
13. hurricane

A. fall (down)

B. have a heart attack

C. drown

D. swallow poison

E. choke

1. car
2. bus
3. truck
4. van
5. motorcycle
6. taxi(cab)/cab

7. subway
8. plane
9. train
10. ship
11. bicycle

1. license plate
2. headlights
3. battery
4. hood
5. windshield
6. trunk
7. gas tank
8. tire

9. dashboard
10. steering wheel
11. ignition
12. brake
13. accelerator / gas pedal
14. seat belt
15. car seat

1. over the highway
2. to / toward the city
3. from / away from the city
4. through the bank

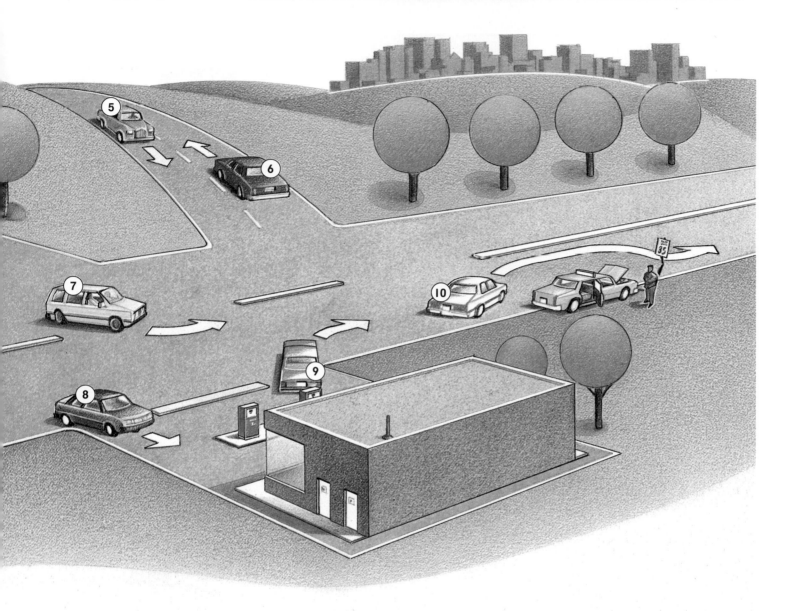

5. down the hill
6. up the hill
7. across the traffic

8. into the gas station
9. out of the gas station
10. around the accident

1. passenger
2. ticket
3. suitcase/luggage
4. security check
5. boarding pass

6. gate
7. flight attendant
8. pilot
9. baggage claim

A. check bags
B. leave/depart
C. wave (good-bye)
D. arrive

E. meet
F. shake hands
G. hug

1. pharmacist / druggist
2. drugstore
3. mechanic
4. attendant
5. service station /
   gas station

6. butcher
7. butcher shop
8. hairdresser / hairstylist
9. beauty salon
10. barber
11. barbershop

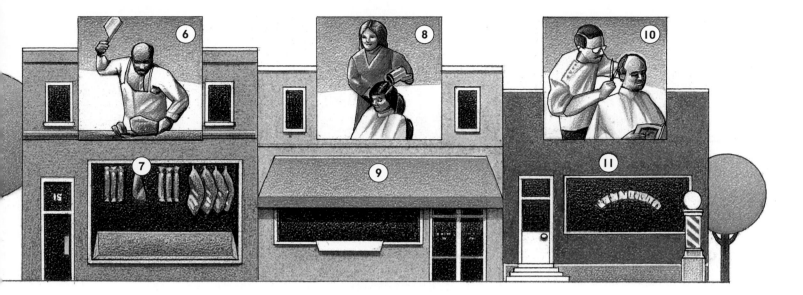

12. librarian
13. library
14. dentist
15. dental assistant
16. office

17. grocer
18. fruit and vegetable market
19. sanitation worker
20. delivery person

1. plumber
2. electrician
3. locksmith
4. housekeeper
5. gardener
6. painter
7. construction worker

8. janitor / custodian
9. mover
10. superintendent / apartment manager
11. doorman
12. taxi driver

13. factory worker
14. foreman
15. bus driver
16. carpenter
17. maintenance man
18. fisherman

19. truck driver
20. farmer
21. soldier
22. sewing machine operator
23. (train) conductor

1. secretary
2. typist/word processor
3. file clerk
4. computer programmer
5. messenger
6. photographer
7. reporter
8. businessman/
   businesswoman
9. accountant
10. lawyer
11. salesperson
12. babysitter
13. dancer
14. singer
15. actor/actress
16. artist

A. take out
B. put in
C. dig
D. oversee
E. lay
F. pour

G. measure
H. hammer
I. climb
J. scrape
K. paint

A. fix / repair TVs / appliances
B. fix / repair cars
C. fix / repair pipes
D. cut hair
E. cut meat

F. cut grass
G. sell clothes
H. sell vegetables
I. sell newspapers
J. build houses
K. build furniture

L. take care of children
M. take care of pools
N. take care of grounds
O. drive a bus
P. drive a cab
Q. drive a truck

R. deliver mail
S. deliver groceries
T. deliver packages
U. collect garbage
V. collect fares
W. collect tickets

1. day-care worker /
   child-care worker
2. stroller
3. pacifier
4. bottle
5. nipple
6. diaper

7. toy
8. bib
9. playpen
10. crib
11. rattle
12. cradle

A. bring/drop off
B. change diapers
C. play
D. crawl
E. run
F. feed

G. take a nap
H. rock
I. hold
J. cry
K. pick up
L. dress

Outdoor Activities

A. go camping
B. go hiking

Sports

C. play tennis
D. play football
E. play basketball
F. play soccer
G. play baseball
H. go skiing

Indoor Activities
I. play an instrument
J. go to the movies
K. watch TV
L. listen to music

Exercise
M. go swimming
N. go running

New Year's Eve
A. drink champagne
B. make a toast

Valentine's Day
C. give valentines
D. get flowers

Easter
E. paint Easter eggs
F. go on an Easter egg hunt

Memorial Day
G. wave a flag
H. watch a parade
I. visit a cemetery

Fourth of July
J. have a barbecue/picnic
K. watch fireworks

Halloween
L. carve out a pumpkin
M. wear a costume
N. go trick-or-treating

Thanksgiving
O. get together with family and friends
P. give thanks
Q. eat a big meal

Christmas
R. send cards
S. go Christmas shopping
T. decorate the tree

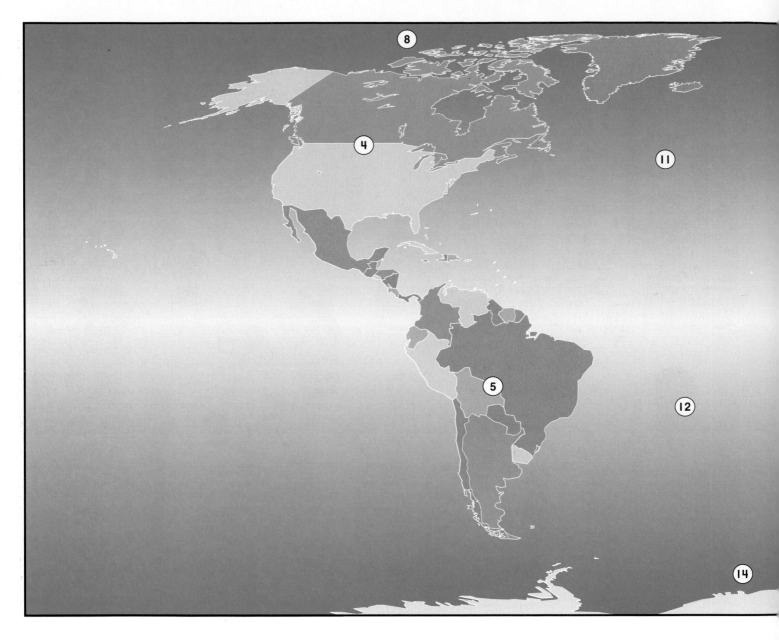

Continents
1. Asia
2. Africa
3. Europe
4. North America
5. South America
6. Australia
7. Antarctica

Oceans
8. Arctic
9. North Pacific
10. South Pacific
11. North Atlantic
12. South Atlantic
13. Indian
14. Antarctic

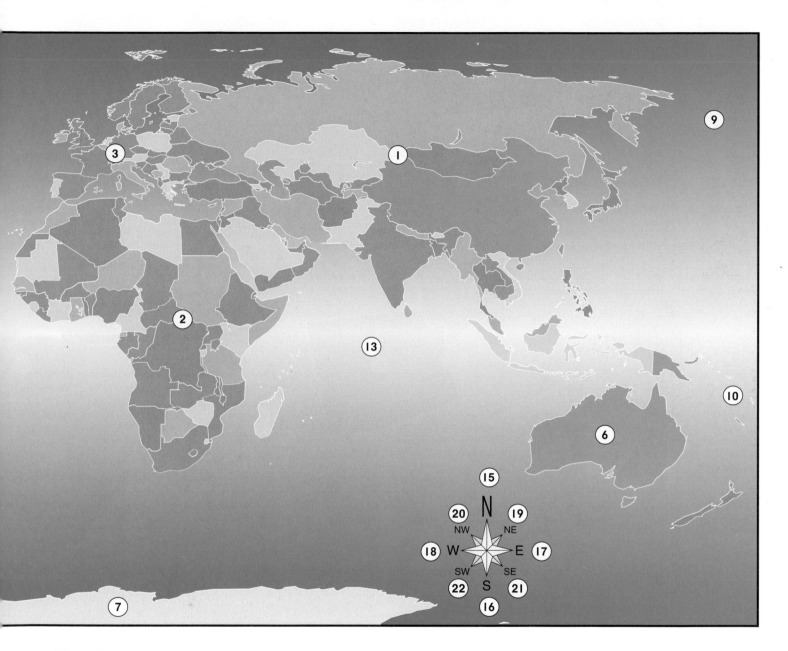

Directions

15. north
16. south
17. east
18. west
19. northeast
20. northwest
21. southeast
22. southwest

1.	Alabama	9.	Florida	17.	Kentucky	25.	Missouri
2.	Alaska	10.	Georgia	18.	Louisiana	26.	Montana
3.	Arizona	11.	Hawaii	19.	Maine	27.	Nebraska
4.	Arkansas	12.	Idaho	20.	Maryland	28.	Nevada
5.	California	13.	Illinois	21.	Massachusetts	29.	New Hampshire
6.	Colorado	14.	Indiana	22.	Michigan	30.	New Jersey
7.	Connecticut	15.	Iowa	23.	Minnesota	31.	New Mexico
8.	Delaware	16.	Kansas	24.	Mississippi	32.	New York

33.	North Carolina	41.	South Dakota	49.	Wisconsin
34.	North Dakota	42.	Tennessee	50.	Wyoming
35.	Ohio	43.	Texas	51.	District of
36.	Oklahoma	44.	Utah		Columbia
37.	Oregon	45.	Vermont		
38.	Pennsylvania	46.	Virginia		
39.	Rhode Island	47.	Washington		
40.	South Carolina	48.	West Virginia		

1	one	1st	first
2	two	2nd	second
3	three	3rd	third
4	four	4th	fourth
5	five	5th	fifth
6	six	6th	sixth
7	seven	7th	seventh
8	eight	8th	eighth
9	nine	9th	ninth
10	ten	10th	tenth
11	eleven		
12	twelve		
13	thirteen		
14	fourteen		
15	fifteen		
16	sixteen		
17	seventeen		
18	eighteen		
19	nineteen		
20	twenty		
21	twenty-one		
30	thirty		
40	forty		
50	fifty		
60	sixty		
70	seventy		
80	eighty		
90	ninety		
100	a/one hundred		
500	five hundred		
621	six hundred (and) twenty-one		
1,000	a/one thousand		
1,000,000	a/one million		

Abbreviations

ounces	oz
teaspoon	tsp
tablespoon	tbs
pint	pt
quart	qt
gallon	gal
pound(s)	lb(s)
inch	in
foot/feet	ft
yard(s)	yd(s)
mile	mi

liter	l
milliliter	ml
gram	g
milligram	mg
kilogram	kg
meter	m
centimeter	cm
kilometer	km

Length, Height, and Distance

ruler

yardstick

measuring tape

1 ft	12 in
1 yd	3 ft
1 mi	1,760 yds

1 in	2.54 cm
1 ft	30.48 cm
1 yd	.941 m
1 mi	1.609 km

Liquid Measure

teaspoon   tablespoon

cup   a quarter cup

a third of a cup   a half cup

1 oz	29.6 ml
1 c	236.5 ml
1 pt	473 ml
1 qt	1.101 l
1/2 gal	1.893 l
1 gal	3.786 l

1 tbs	3 tsp	1/2 oz
1 c	16 tbs	8 oz
1 pt	2 c	16 oz
1 qt	2 pt	32 oz
1/2 gal	2 qt	64 oz
1 gal	2 qt	64 oz

Solid Weights

1 lb	454 g
1 kg	2.205 lbs

Abbreviations

degrees Fahrenheit	°F
degrees Celsius/Centigrade	°C

From Fahrenheit to Centigrade/Celsius

subtract 32, multiply by 5, divide by 9

50°F   50
       -32

        $18 \times 5 = 90$

        $90 \div 9 = 10°C$

From Centigrade/Celsius to Fahrenheit:

multiply by 9, divide by 5, add 32

10°C $10 \times 9 =$ 90

           $90 \div 5 =$ 18
                 +32
                 50°F

Two numbers occur after words in the index: the first refers to the page where the word is illustrated and the second to the item number of the word on that page. For example, above [ə bŭv**ʹ**] **54**/1 means that the word *above* is the item numbered 1 on page 54. If only a bold number appears, then that word is part of the unit title or a subtitle.

The index includes a pronunciation guide for all the words illustrated in the book. This guide uses symbols commonly found in dictionaries for native speakers. These symbols, unlike those used in transcription systems such as the International Phonetic Alphabet, tend to preserve spelling and so should help you to become more aware of the connections between written English and spoken English.

Consonants

[b] as in **back** [băk]	[k] as in **kiss** [kĭs]	[sh] as in **ship** [shĭp]
[ch] as in **cheek** [chēk]	[l] as in **leg** [lĕg]	[t] as in **tape** [tāp]
[d] as in **date** [dāt]	[m] as in **man** [măn]	[th] as in **three** [thrē]
[dh] as in **the** [dh]	[n] as in **neck** [nĕk]	[v] as in **vest** [vĕst]
[f] as in **face** [fās]	[ng] as in **ring** [rĭng]	[w] as in **waist** [wāst]
[g] as in **gas** [găs]	[p] as in **pack** [păk]	[y] as in **yard** [yärd]
[h] as in **half** [hăf]	[r] as in **rake** [rāk]	[z] as in **zip** [zĭp]
[j] as in **jeans** [jēnz]	[s] as in **sad** [săd]	[zh] as in **measure** [mĕzh**ʹ**ər]

Vowels

[ā] as in **bake** [bāk]	[ī] as in **lime** [līm]	[o͞o] as in **cool** [ko͞ol]
[ă] as in **back** [băk]	[ĭ] as in **lip** [lĭp]	[o͝o] as in **book** [bo͝ok]
[ä] as in **bar** [bär]	[ï] as in **heel** [hïl]	[ow] as in **brown** [brown]
[ē] as in **bean** [bēn]	[ō] as in **post** [pōst]	[oy] as in **boy** [boy]
[ĕ] as in **bed** [bĕd]	[ŏ] as in **box** [bŏks]	[ŭ] as in **cut** [kŭt]
[ë] as in **pear** [për]	[ö] as in **lawn** [lön]	[ü] as in **curb** [kürb]
	or **for** [för]	[ə] as in **above** [ə bŭv**ʹ**]

All pronunciation symbols used are alphabetical except for the schwa [ə], which is the most frequent vowel sound in English. If you use it appropriately in unstressed syllables, your pronunciation will sound more natural.

You should note that an umlaut ([¨]) calls attention to the special quality of vowels before [r]. (The sound [ö] can also represent a vowel not followed by [r] as in *lawn*.) You should listen carefully to native speakers to discover how these vowels actually sound.

Stress

This guide also follows the system for marking stress used in many dictionaries for native speakers.
   (1) Stress is not marked if a word consisting of a single syllable occurs in isolation.
   (2) Where stress is marked, two levels are distinguished:
       a bold accent [**ʹ**] is placed after each syllable with primary stress.
       a light accent [ʹ] is placed after each syllable with secondary stress.

Syllable Boundaries

Syllable boundaries are indicated by a single space.

NOTE: The pronunciation used in this index is based on patterns of American English. There has been no attempt to represent all of the varieties of American English. Students should listen to native speakers to hear how the language actually sounds in a particular region.

A

Abbreviations [ə brē′vē ā′shənz] 101
above [ə bŭv′] 54/1
accelerator [ăk sĕl′ə rā′tər] 77/13
Accessories [ăk sĕs′ə rēz] 55
accident [ăk′sə dənt] 74/4
accountant [ə kown′tənt] 86/9
Aches [āks] 62–63
across [ə krös′] 79/7
Activities, Indoor [ĭn′dör′ ăk tĭv′ə tēz] 93
Activities, Outdoor
    [owt′dör′ ăk tĭv′ə tēz] 92
actor [ăk′tər] 86/15
actress [ăk′trəs] 86/15
address [ă′drəs] 71/9
address, return [rə türn′ ə drĕs′] 71/7
adult [ə dŭlt′] 11/8
Africa [ă′frĭ kə] 96/2
afternoon [ăf′tər nōōn′] 6/2
Age [āj] 13
air conditioner [ër′ kən dĭ′shə nər] 26/4
Airport [ër′pört′] 80–81
aisle [ī′əl] 40/2
Alabama [ăl′ə bă′mə] 98/1
alarm clock [ə lärm′ klök′] 26/13
Alaska [ə lăs′kə] 98/2
alter [öl′tər] 57/D
alterations [öl′tə rā′shənz] 57/D
ambulance [ăm′byə ləns] 74/5
America, North [nörth′ ə mër′ə kə] 96/4
America, South [sowth′ ə mër′ə kə] 96/5
amount [ə mownt′] 70/8
angry [ăng′grē] 18/1
ankle [ăng′kəl] 59/20
ankle, swollen [swō′lən ăng′kəl] 63/15
Antarctic Ocean [ănt ärk′tĭk ō′shən] 96/14
Antarctica [ănt ärk′tĭ kə] 96/7
Apartment Building
    [ə pärt′mənt bĭl′dĭng] 23
apartment manager
    [ə pärt′mənt măn′ĭ jər] 84/10
apple pie [ă′pəl pī′] 45/22
apples [ă′pəlz] 35/3
appliances, fix [fĭks′ ə plī′əns əz] 88/A
appliances, repair [rə për′ ə plī′əns əz] 88/A
April [ā′prəl] 4/4
Arctic Ocean [ärk′tĭk ō′shən] 96/8
Arizona [ăr′ə zō′nə] 98/3
Arkansas [är′kən sö′] 98/4
arm [ärm] 58/12
arm, broken [brō′kən ärm′] 63/14

armchair [ärm′chër′] 24/5
around [ə rownd′] 79/10
arrive [ə rīv′] 81/D
artist [är′təst] 86/18
Asia [ā′zhə] 96/1
At the store [ăt dhə stör′] 54
athletic shoes [ăth lĕ′tĭk shōōz′] 49/8
Atlantic Ocean, North
    [nörth′ ăt lăn′tĭk ō′shən] 96/11
Atlantic Ocean, South
    [sowth′ ăt lăn′tĭk ō′shən] 96/12
ATM machine [ā′tē ĕm′ mə shēn′] 70/4
attendant [ə tĕn′dənt] 82/4
attendant, flight [flīt′ ə tĕn′dənt] 80/7
August [ö′gəst] 4/8
aunt [ănt] 16/7
Australia [ö strāl′yə] 96/6
average height [ăv′rəj hīt′] 12/2
average weight [ăv′rəj wāt′] 12/5
away from [ə wā′ frŭm] 78/3

B

baby [bā′bē] 11/1
baby, have a [hăv′ ə bā′bē] 21/1
babysitter [bā′bē sĭt′ ər] 86/12
back [băk] 59/15
backache [băk′āk′] 62/4
backpack [băk′păk′] 50/6
backyard [băk′yärd′] 22/12
bacon [bā′kən] 36/5
bag [băg] 40/11, 55/5
bag of flour [băg′ əv flow′ər] 37/6
baggage claim [băg′ ĭj klām′] 80/9
bagger [băg′ər] 40/12
bags, check [chĕk băgz′] 81/A
bake a casserole [bāk′ ə kăs′ə rōl] 47/L
baked potato [bākt′ pə tā′tō] 45/17
bakery [bă′kə rē] 68/10
balcony [băl′kə nē] 23/1
bald [böld] 13/13
bananas [bə nă′nəz] 35/1
bandage [băn′dĭj] 65/2
Ban-Aid [bănd′ād′] 65/1
Banking [băng′kĭng] 70
bar of soap [bär′ əv sōp′] 37/11
barbeque, have a [hăv′ ə bär′bə kyōō′] 95/J
barber [bär′bər] 82/10
barber shop [bär′bər shöp′] 82/11
baseball, play [plā′ bās böl′] 92/G
baseball cap [bās′ böl kăp′] 49/6
basement [bās′mənt] 23/7

basement, flooded [flŭ′əd băs′mənt] 49/6

basket, laundry [lön′drē băs′kət] 56/5

basket, shopping [shŏp′ ĭng băs′kət] 40/3

basketball, play [plā′ băs′kət böl′] 92/E

bathing suit [bā′dhĭng sōot′] 49/1-2

bathrobe [băth′rōb′] 51/11

Bathroom [băth′rōōm′] 27

bathroom, clean the
  [klēn dhə băth′rōōm′] 28/C

bathtub [băth′tŭb′] 27/5

battery [băt′ə rē] 77/3

be born [bē′ börn′] 20/A

beans [bēnz] 39/16

beard [bïrd] 13/9

beauty salon [byōō′tē să lön′] 82/9

bed [běd] 26/7

bed, go to [gō′ tə běd′] 15/O

bed, make the [māk′ dhə běd′] 28/A

Bedroom [běd′rōōm′] 26

bedspread [běd′ sprěd′] 26/10

beef [bēf] 36/1

behind [bə hīnd′] 54/8

beige [bāzh] 9/14

bell pepper [běl′ pěp′ər] 34/9

below [bə lō′] 54/2

belt [bělt] 48/6

bench [běnch] 72/12

between [bə twēn′] 54/4

bib [bĭb] 90/8

bicycle [bī sĭ kəl] 76/11

big [bĭg] 12/7

bill [bĭl] 10/11

bills [bĭlz] 10/1

Birthday Party [bürth′dā pär′tē] 17

black [blăk] 9/4

black hair [blăk′ hër′] 13/20

blades [blādz] 61/9

blanket [blăng′kət] 26/11

blond hair [blŏnd′ hër′] 13/17

blood pressure, high [hī blŭd′ prěsh′ər] 63/13

bloody nose [blŭd′ē nōz′] 63/17

blouse [blows] 48/2

blow out the candles
  [blō′ owt dhə kăn′dəlz] 17/F

blue [blōō] 9/7

blue, dark [därk′ blōō′] 9/17

blue, light [līt′ blōō′] 9/16

board [börd] 2/1

boarding pass [bör′ding păs′] 80/5

Body [bŏ′dē] 58-59

boil water [boyl′ wŏ′tər] 46/B

book [bōōk] 2/8

bookcase [bōōk′kās′] 24/12

bookstore [bōōk′stör′] 68/8

booth [bōōth] 43/3

boots [bōōts] 50/7

bored [börd] 18/5

born, be [bē′börn′] 20/A

bottle [bŏt′əl] 90/4

bottle, hot water [hŏt wŏ′tər bŏt′əl] 65/7

bottle of soda [bŏt′əl əv sō′də] 37/3

bottle return [bŏt′əl rētürn′] 40/13

bowl [bōl] 42/4

box of cereal [bŏks′əv sïr′ēəl] 37/10

boxer shorts [bŏk′sər shörts] 51/2

boy [boy] 11/3

bra [brŏ] 51/7

bracelet [brās′lət] 55/2

brain [brān] 59/24

brake [brāk] 77/9

bread [brěd] 38/9

bread, loaf of [lōf′ əv brěd] 37/5

breakfast, eat [ēt′brěk′ fast] 15/I

breast [brěst] 58/13

bring [brĭng] 91/A

broccoli [brŏk′lē] 34/1

broccoli, cut [kŭt′brŏk′lē] 46/C

broil fish [broyl′fĭsh′] 47/M

broiler [broy′lər] 25/8

broken arm [brō′kən ärm′] 63/14

broken lock [brō′kən lŏk′] 32/8

broken steps [brō′kən stěps′] 33/9

broken window [brō′kən wĭn′dō] 32/3

broom [brōōm] 30/2

brother [brŭdh′ər] 16/5

brown [brown] 9/10

brown hair [brown′ hër′] 13/19

bruise [brōōz] 62/9

brush [brŭsh] 30/8, 61/2

brush . . . teeth [brŭsh′ . . . tēth′] 14/D

bucket [bŭk′ət] 30/11

build furniture [bĭld′für′nə chər] 88/K

build houses [bĭld′how′zəz] 88/J

bureau [byōōr′ō] 26/2

burner [bür′nər] 25/4

burn . . . self [bürn′ . . . sĕlf′] 63/D

bus [bŭs] 76/2

bus, drive a [drīv′ə bŭs′] 89/O

bus, wait for the [wāt′ för dhə bŭs′] 73/K

bus driver [bŭs′drī′vər] 85/15

bus station [bŭs′stā′shən] 69/13

bus stop [bŭs′stŏp′] 72/11

busboy [bŭs′ boy′]   43/5
businessman [bĭz′ nəs măn′]   86/8
businessman [bĭz′ nəs wŏŏm′ ən]   86/8
butcher [bŏŏ′ chər]   82/6
butcher shop [bŏŏ′ chər shŏp′]   82/7
butter [bŭt′ ər]   38/6
button [bŭt′ ən]   57/4
buy groceries [bī′ grō′ sə rēz]   73/G

C

cab [kăb]   76/6
cab, drive a [drīv′ ə kăb′]   89/P
cabbage [kăb′ ĭj]   34/2
cabinet [kăb′ ə nət]   25/12
cabinet, medicine
   [mĕd′ ə sən kăb′ ə nət]   27/9
cake, cut the [cŭt′ dhə kāk′]   17/I
Calendar [kăl′ ən dər]   5
calf [kăf]   59/19
California [kăl′ ə för′ nyə]   98/5
camping, go [gō′ kăm′ pĭng]   92/A
can of soup [kăn′ əv sōōp′]   37/8
can opener [kăn′ ō′ pə nər]   25/9
candles, blow out the
   [blō′ owt dhə kăn′ dəlz]   17/F
cap [kăp]   48/10
cap, baseball [bās′ böl kăp′]   49/6
car [kär]   76/1
Car, Parts of a [pärts′ əv ə kär′]   77
car seat [kär′ sēt′]   77/15
card, open a [ō′ pən ə kärd′]   17/J
cards, send [sĕnd′ kärdz′]   95/R
carpenter [kär′ pən tər]   85/16
carpet [kär′ pət]   26/6
carrot [kär′ ət]   34/13
carry [kär′·ē]   41/B
cars, fix [fĭks′ kärz′]   88/B
cars, repair [rə për′ kärz′]   88/B
carton of milk [kär′ tən əv mĭlk]   37/1
carve out a pumpkin
   [kärv′ owt′ ə pŭmp′ kən]   95/L
cash machine [kăsh′ mə shēn′]   70/4
cash register [kăsh′ rĕ′ jə stər]   40/8
cashier [kă shïr′]   43/12
casserole, bake a [bāk′ ə kăs′ ə rōl]   47/L
cast, get a [gĕt′ ə kăst′]   64/E
ceiling [sē′ lĭng]   24/1
ceiling, cracked [krăkt′ sē′ lĭng]   32/4
ceiling, leaking [lē′ kĭng sē′ lĭng]   32/1
Celebrate the Holidays
   [sĕl′ ə brāt dhə hŏl ə dāz]   94–95

cemetery, visit a [vĭz′ ət ə sĕm′ ə tër′ ē]   94/I
centimeter [sĕn′ tə mē′ tər]   101
cents [sĕnts]   10/8
cereal [sïr′ ē əl]   38/10
cereal, box [bŏks′ əv sïr′ ē əl]   37/10
chair [chër]   2/6
chalk [chök]   2/2
chalkboard [chök′ börd′]   2/1
champagne, drink [drĭngk′ shăm pān′]   94/A
change [chānj]   55/7
change diapers [chānj′ dī′ pərz]   91/B
change the sheets [chānj′ dhə shēts′]   29/L
check [chĕk]   10/10, 70/6
check bags [chĕk′ băgz′]   81/A
checker [chĕk′ ər]   40/9
checkout [chĕk′ owt]   40/9
checkout counter [chĕk′ owt kown′ tər]   40/9
checkout person [chĕk′ owt pür′ sən]   40/6
cheek [chēk]   60/8
cheese [chēz]   38/5
cheese, grate [grāt′ chēz′]   46/H
cherries [chër′ ēz]   35/12
chest [chĕst]   58/4
chest, medicine [mĕd′ ə sən chĕst′]   27/9
chicken [chĭk′ ən]   36/8
chicken, fried [frīd′ chĭk′ ən]   45/20
child [chīld]   11/6
child-care worker [chīld′ kër′ wür′ kər]   90/1
children, take care of
   [tāk′ kër′ əv chīl′ drən]   89/L
chimney [chĭm′ nē]   22/1
chin [chĭn]   60/7
choke [chōk]   75/E
choose [chōōz]   41/D
chop peppers [chŏp′ pĕp′ ərz]   46/E
Christmas [krĭs′ məs]   95
Christmas shopping, go
   [gō′ krĭs′ məs shŏp′ ĭng]   95/E
church [chürch]   68/6
circle [sür′ kəl]   9/1
city hall [sĭ′ tē höl′]   69/12
clams [klămz]   36/13
Classroom [klăs′ rōōm]   2–3
clean [klēn]   52/5
clean the bathroom
   [klēn′ dhə băth′ rōōm′]   28/C
Cleaning Implements
   [klēn′ ĭng ĭm′ plə mənts]   30
cleanser [klĕn′ zər]   30/6
climb [klīm]   87/I
clock [klŏk]   7/1

clock, alarm [ə lärm′ klŏk′]   26/13
clogged drain [klŏgd′ drān′]   33/11
close the window [klōz′ dhə wĭn′ dō]   3/I
closet [klŏz′ ət]   26/1
cloth [klŏth]   30/5
Clothes, Basic [bā′ sĭk klŏz′]   48
Clothes, Casual [kăzh′ ə wəl klŏz′]   49
Clothes, Cold Weather
   [kōld′ wĕdh′ ər klŏz′]   50
Clothes, Describing [dĭs krī′ bĭng klŏz′]   52–53
clothes, look at the [lŏŏk′ ăt dhə klŏz′]   73/H
clothes, sell [sĕl′ klŏz′]   88/G
Clothes, Taking Care of
   [tā′ kĭng kër əv klŏz′]   56–57
cloudy [klow′ dē]   8/5
coat [kōt]   50/11
cockroaches [kŏk′ rōch əz]   33/13
coffee [kö′ fē]   38/11
coffee, jar of [jär′ əv kö′ fē]   37/7
coffee table [kö′ fē tā′ bəl]   24/9
coins [koynz]   10/3
cold [kōld]   8/12, 62/1
collect fares [kə lĕkt′ fërz′]   89/V
collect garbage [kə lĕkt′ gär′ bĭj]   89/U
collect tickets [kə lĕkt′ tĭk′ əts]   89/W
Colorado [kŏl′ ə rŏd′ ō]   98/6
Colors [kŭl′ ərz]   9
comb [kōm]   61/1
comb . . . hair [kōm′ . . . hër′]   14/F
come home [kŭm′ hōm′]   15/M
come in [kŭm′ in′]   3/D
come out of the store
   [kŭm owt′ əv dhə stör′]   73/A
Community [kə myōō′ nə tē]   68–69
computer [kəm pyōō′ tər]   2/13
computer, work at the
   [würk′ ăt dhə kəm pyōō′ tər]   3/G
computer programmer
   [kəm pyōō′ tər prō′ grăm ər]   86/4
conductor [kən dŭk′ tər]   85/23
Connecticut [kə nĕ′ tĭ kət]   98/7
Construction Site [kən strŭk′ shən sīt′]   87
construction worker
   [kən strŭk′ shən wür′ kər]   84/7
container of yogurt
   [kən tā′ nər əv yō′ gərt]   37/2
Continents [kŏn′ tə nənts]   96
cook [kŏŏk]   43/1
cook dinner [kŏŏk′ dĭn′ ər]   15/N
cookies [kŏŏk′ ēz]   39/21

cookies, package of
   [păk′ ĭj əv kŏŏk′ ēz]   37/4
Cooking a Meal [kŏŏk′ ĭng ə mēl′]   46–47
cool [kŏŏl]   8/11
corn [körn]   34/5
corner [kör′ nər]   72/5
costume, wear a [wër′ ə kŏs′ tōōm]   95/M
cotton balls [kŏ′ tən bölz′]   65/4
couch [kowch]   24/11
cough [köf]   63/B
counter [kown′ tər]   25/14
courthouse [kört′ hows′]   68/3
cousins [kŭz′ ənz]   16/8
cracked ceiling [krăkt′ sē′ lĭng]   32/4
cracked wall [krăkt′ wöl]   32/2
cradle [krā′ dəl]   90/12
crawl [kröl]   91/D
cream [krēm]   38/2, 64/3
credit card [krĕd′ ĭt kärd′]   10/9
crib [krĭb]   90/10
cross the street [krös′ dhə strēt′]   73/E
crosswalk [krös′ wök′]   72/3
crutches [krŭch′ əz]   65/8
cry [krī]   91/J
cucumber [kyōō′ kŭm bər]   34/10
cup [kŭp] .   42/7, 101
cup, a half [ə hăf′ kŭp′]   101
cup, a quarter [ə kwör′ tər kŭp′]   101
cup, a third of a [ə thürd′ əv ə kŭp′]   101
curb [kürb]   72/10
curly hair [kür′ lē hër′]   13/16
curtain, shower [show′ ər kür′ tən]   27/2
curtains [kür′ tənz]   26/5
custodian [kŭs tō′ dē ən]   84/8
customer [kŭs tə′ mər]   40/5
cut [kŭt]   62/8
cut broccoli [kŭt′ brŏk′ lē]   46/C
cut grass [kŭt′ grăs′]   88/F
cut hair [kŭt′ hër′]   88/D
cut meat [kŭt′ mēt′]   88/E
cut the cake [kŭt′ dhə kāk′]   17/I

D

Daily Routines [dā′ lē rōō tēnz′]   14–15
Dairy Products [dër′ ē prŏd′ ŭkts]   38–39
dancer [dăn′ sər]   86/13
dark blue [därk′ blōō′]   9/17
dashboard [dăsh′ börd′]   77/9
date [dāt]   70/7
daughter [dö′ tər]   16/13
day [dā]   5/14

Day, Times of [tīmz′ əv dā′]	6
Day-Care Center [dā′kër′ sĕn′tər]	90–91
day-care worker [dā′kër′ wür′kər]	90/I
December [dē sĕm′bər]	4/12
deck [dĕk]	22/10
decorate the tree [dĕk′ə rāt dhə trē′]	95/T
Delaware [dĕl′ə wär′]	98/8
deliver groceries [də lĭv′ər grō′sə rēz]	89/S
deliver mail [də lĭv′ər māl′]	89/R
deliver packages [də lĭv′ər păk′ĭj əz]	89/T
delivery person [də lĭv′ər ē pür′sən]	83/20
dental assistant [dĕn′təl ə sĭs′tənt]	83/15
dentist [dĕn′tĭst]	83/14
deodorant [dē ōd′ə rənt]	61/10
depart [də pärt′]	81/B
Department of Motor Vehicles	
[də pärt′mənt əv mō′tər vē′ə kəlz]	69/16
department store [də pärt′mənt stör′]	69/20
deposit slip [də pŏz′ət slĭp′]	70/11
Describing Clothes [də skrī′bĭng klōz′]	52–53
Describing People [də skrī′bĭng pē′pəl]	12–13
desk [dĕsk]	2/7
detergent [dĭ tür′jənt]	56/2
diaper [dī′pər]	90/6
diapers, change [chānj′ dī′pərz]	91/B
die [dī]	21/L
diet, go on a [gō′ ŏn ə dī′ət]	64/G
dig [dĭg]	87/C
dime [dīm]	10/6
dinner, cook [kook′ dĭn′ər]	15/N
Directions [dĭ rĕk′shənz]	97
dirty [dür′tē]	52/6
dishes, dry the [drī′ dhə dĭsh′əz]	28/G
dishes, wash the [wŏsh′ dhə dĭsh′əz]	28/F
dishwasher [dĭsh′wŏsh′ər]	43/2
Distance [dĭs′təns]	101
District of Columbia	
[dĭs′trĭkt əv kə lŭm′bē ə]	99/51
divorced, get	
[gĕt′ dĭ′vörst]	21/H
DMV	
[dē ĕm vē′]	69/16
do alterations [doo′ öl′tə rā′shənz]	57/D
do the laundry [doo′ dhə lön′drē]	29/P
doctor [dŏk′tər]	66/6
dollar [dŏl′ər]	10/2
donuts [dō′nŭts]	44/9
door, front [frŭnt′ dör′]	22/4
doorman [dör′mān′]	84/11
down [down]	79/5
down vest [down′ vĕst′]	50/2
drain [drān]	27/4
drain, clogged [klŏgd′ drān′]	33/11
drapes [drāps]	24/4
drawer [drör]	26/3
dress [drĕs]	48/1, 91/L
dresser [drĕs′ər]	26/2
dried beans [drīd′ bēnz′]	39/16
drill [drĭl]	31/6
drink champagne [drĭngk′ shăm pān′]	94/A
drink milk [drĭngk′ mĭlk′]	17/H
dripping faucet [drĭp′ĭng fö′sĭt]	33/10
drive a bus [drīv′ ə bŭs′]	89/O
drive a cab [drīv′ ə kăb′]	89/P
drive a truck [drīv′ ə trŭk′]	89/Q
driver, bus [bŭs′drī′vər]	85/15
driver, taxi [tăk′sī drī′vər]	84/12
driver, truck [trŭk′drī′vər]	85/19
drive-thru window [drīv′throo wĭn′dō]	70/2
driveway [drīv′wā′]	22/7
drop off [drŏp′ öf′]	91/A
dropper, medicine [mĕd′ə sən drŏp′ər]	64/6
drops [drŏps]	64/5
drown [drown]	75/C
druggist [drŭg′ĭst]	82/1
drugs [drŭgz]	64/1
drugstore [drŭg′stör′]	82/2
dry [drī]	53/12
Dry Cleaner [drī′klē′nər]	57
dry the dishes [drī′ dhə dĭsh′əz]	28/G
dry [drī′ər]	56/3
dust the furniture [dŭst′ dhə für′nə chər]	28/E
dustpan [dŭst′ păn′]	30/3
E	
ear [ïr]	60/3
earache [ïr′āk′]	62/7
earmuffs [ïr′mŭfs′]	50/14
earrings [ïr′ĭngz]	55/3
earthquake [ürth′kwāk′]	74/11
east [ēst]	97/17
Easter [ē′stər]	94
Easter egg hunt, go on an	
[gō′ ŏn ən ē′stər ĕg hŭnt′]	94/F
Easter eggs, paint	
[pānt′ ē′stər ĕgz′]	94/E
easy chair [ē′zē chër′]	24/5
eat a big meal [ēt′ ə bĭg′ mēl′]	95/Q
eat breakfast [ēt′ brĕk′fəst]	15/I
eggs [ĕgz]	38/4
eggs, fried [frīd′ ĕgz′]	44/3
eggs, scrambled [skrăm′bəld ĕgz′]	44/1

elbow [ĕl′bō]	59/17
electrician [ĭ lĕk trĭ′shən]	84/2
elevator [ĕl′ə vā′tər]	23/10
embarrassed [ĭm băr′əst]	19/13
Emergencies [ĭ mür′jən sēz]	74–75
empty the wastebasket [ĕm′tē dhə wāst′băs′kət]	29/K
end table [ĕnd′ tā′bəl]	24/8
English muffin [ĭng′lĭsh mŭf′ən]	44/5
entrance [ĕn′trəns]	23/5
envelope [ĕn′və lōp′]	71/6
eraser [ĭ rā′sər]	2/3
Europe [yŏŏr′əp]	96/3
evening [ēv′nĭng]	6/3
examine the patient [ĭg zăm′ĭn dhə pā′shənt]	67/F
examining room [ĭg zăm′ə nĭng rōōm′]	66/8
excited [ĭk sīt′əd]	18/7
exercise [ĕk′sər sīz]	64/F, 93
exit [ĕg′zĭt]	23/4
extra-large [ĕk′strə lärj′]	53/20
eye [ī]	60/5
eyebrow [ī′brow′]	60/4
F	
face [fās]	58/1, 60
factory worker [făk′tə rē würk′ər]	85/13
faint [fānt]	63/C
fall [föl]	4/16, 75/A
fall down [föl′ down′]	75/A
fall in love [föl′ ĭn lŭv′]	21/F
Family [făm′ə lē]	16
family and friends, get together with [gĕt′ tə gĕdh′ər wĭth făm′lē ănd frĕndz′]	95/O
fares, collect [kə lĕkt′ fĕrz′]	89/V
farmer [färm′ər]	85/20
fat [făt]	12/4
father [fŏdh′ər]	16/2
faucet [fö′sĭt]	27/3
faucet, dripping [drĭp′ĭng fö′sĭt]	33/10
February [fĕb′rōō ĕr′ē]	4/2
feed [fēd]	91/F
feelings [fē′lĭngz]	18–19
fever [fē′vər]	62/2
file clerk [fīl′ klürk′]	86/3
fill out the form [fĭl′ owt′ dhə förm′]	67/A
finger [fĭng′gər]	58/8
fire [fīr]	74/2
fire escape [fīr′ə skāp′]	23/3
fire exit [fīr′ ĕg′zĭt]	23/4
fire fighter [fīr′ fī′tər]	74/3
firehouse [fīr′hows′]	68/2
fireworks, watch [wŏch′ fīr′würks′]	95/K
First Aid [fürsl′ ād′]	65
fish [fĭsh]	36/10
fish, broil [broyl′ fĭsh′]	47/M
fisherman [fĭsh′ər mən]	85/18
fix appliances [fĭks′ ə plī′əns əz]	88/A
fix cars [fĭks′ kärz′]	88/B
fix pipes [fĭks′ pīps′]	88/C
fix TVs [fĭks′ tē vēz′]	88/A
flag, wave a [wāv′ ə flăg′]	94/G
flashlight [flăsh′ līt′]	31/8
flight attendant [flīt′ ə tĕn′ dənt]	80/7
flood [flŭd]	74/10
flooded basement [flŭd′əd bās′mənt]	33/15
floor [flör]	23/2, 24/3
floor, mop the [mŏp′ dhə flör′]	29/O
floor, sweep the [swēp′ dhə flör′]	29/M
Florida [flör′ə də]	98/9
florist [flör′ĭst]	68/9
flour [flow′ər]	38/13
flour, bag of [băg′ əv flow′ər]	37/6
flowers, get [gĕt′ flow′ərz]	94/D
foggy [fŏg′ē]	8/7
fold [fōld]	56/D
food [fōōd]	34–39
Foods, Prepared [prē pĕrd′ fōōdz′]	44–45
foot [fōōt]	59/21
football, play [plā′ fōōt′böl′]	92/D
foot/feet [fōōt] [fēt]	101
forehead [för′hĕd′]	60/2
foreman [för′mən]	85/14
fork [förk]	42/11
form, fill out the [fĭl′ owt′ dhə förm′]	67/A
Fourth of July [förth′ əv jōō lī′]	95
freezer [frē′zər]	25/15
freezing [frē′zĭng]	8/13
french fries [frĕnch′ frīz′]	44/12
Friday [frī′dā]	5/6
fried chicken [frīd′ chĭk′ən]	45/20
fried eggs [frīd′ĕgz′]	44/3
friends, get together with family and [gĕt′ tə gĕdh′ər wĭth făm′ lē ănd frĕndz′]	95/O
from [frŭm]	78/3
front door [frŭnt′ dör′]	22/4
fruit and vegetable market [frōōt′ ănd vej′tə bəl mär′kət]	83/18
fruits [frōōts]	35

fry onions and peppers
 [frī′ ŭn′yənz ănd pĕp′ərz] 46/F
frying pan [frī′ĭng păn′] 25/5
furniture, build [bĭld′ für′nə chər] 88/K
furniture, dust the [dŭst′ dhə für′nə chər] 28/E

G
gallon [găl′ən] 101
garage [gə rŏj′] 22/6
garage, parking [pär′kĭng gə rŏj′] 69/15
garbage, collect [kə lĕkt′ gär′bĭj] 89/U
garbage, take out the
 [tāk′ owt′ dhə gär′bĭj] 28/J
garbage can [gär′bĭj kăn′] 22/9
garden [gär′dən] 22/13
gardener [gärd′nər] 84/5
garlic [gär′lĭk] 34/6
gas pedal [găs′ pĕd′əl] 77/13
gas station [găs′ stā′shən] 82/5
gas tank [găs′ tănk′] 77/7
gate [gāt] 80/6
Georgia [jör′jə] 98/10
get a cast [gĕt′ ə kăst′] 64/E
get a job [gĕt′ ə jŏb′] 20/D
get divorced [gĕt′ dĭ vörst′] 21/H
get dressed [gĕt′ drĕst′] 14/H
get flowers [gĕt′ flow′ərz] 94/D
get married [gĕt′ măr′ēd] 21/G
get rest [gĕt′ rĕst′] 64/B
get sick [gĕt′ sĭk′] 21/K
get stitches [gĕt′ stĭch′əz] 64/C
get together with family and friends
 [gĕt′ tə gĕdh′ər wĭth
 făm′lē ănd frĕndz′] 95/O
get up [gĕt ′up′] 14/B
girl [gürl] 11/2
give a present to [gĭv′ ə prĕz′ənt tōō] 17/A
give a shot [gĭv′ ə shŏt′] 67/I
give an injection [gĭv′ ən ĭn jĕk′shən] 67/I
give thanks [gĭv′ thănks′] 95/P
give valentines [gĭv′ văl′ən tīnz] 94/C
glass [glăs] 42/6
glasses [glăs′əz] 55/8
gloves [glŭvz] 50/13
gloves, rubber [rŭb′ər glŭvz′] 30/7
go camping [gō′ kăm′pĭng] 92/A
go Christmas shopping
 [gō′ krĭs′məs shŏp′ĭng] 95/S
go hiking [gō′ hī′kĭng] 92/B
go into the store [gō′ ĭn tə dhə stör′] 73/B
go on a diet [gō′ ŏn ə dī′ət] 64/G

go on an Easter egg hunt
 [gō′ ŏn ən ē′stər ĕg hŭnt′] 94/F
go out [gō′ owt′] 3/C
go running [gō′ rŭn′ĭng] 93/N
go skiing [gō′ skē′ĭng] 92/H
go swimming [gō′ swĭ′mĭng] 93/M
go to bed [gō′ tə bĕd′] 15/O
go to sleep [gō′ tə slēp′] 15/P
go to the movies [gō′ tə dhə mōō′vēz] 93/J
go trick-or-treating [gō′ trĭk ər trē′tĭng] 95/N
good-bye, wave [wāv′ gōōd bī′] 81/C
graduate [grăj′ə wāt′] 20/C
gram [grăm] 101
grand parents [grănd′ păr′ənts] 16/I
grapefruit [grāp′frōōt′] 35/6
grapes [grāps] 35/2
grass, cut [kŭt′grăs′] 88/F
grate cheese [grāt′chēz′] 46/H
gray [grā] 9/11
gray hair [grā′ hër′] 13/21
green [grēn] 9/9
grocer [grō′sər] 83/17
groceries [grō′sə rēz] 40/10
groceries, buy [bī′ grō′sə rēz] 73/G
groceries, deliver [də lĭv′ər grō′sə rēz] 89/S
ground meat [grownd′ mēt′] 36/3
grounds, take care of
 [tāk′ kër′ əv growndz′] 89/N

H
Hair 13
hair [hër] 60/1
hair, cut [kŭt′ hër′] 88/D
hairdresser [hër′drĕs′ər] 82/8
hairstylist [hër′stī′lĭst] 82/8
half cup, a [ə hăf′ kŭp′] 101
hall [höl] 23/8
Halloween [hŏl′ə wēn′] 95
ham [hăm] 36/6
hamburger [hăm′bür′gər] 44/11
hammer [hăm′ər] 31/4, 87/H
hamper [hăm′pər] 27/10
hand [hănd] 58/5
hands, shake [shāk′ hăndz′] 81/F
hang up [hăng′ ŭp′] 57/B
hanger [hăng′ər] 57/9
happy [hăp′ē] 18/2
hat [hăt] 50/4
have a baby [hăv′ ə bā′bē] 21/I
have a barbecue [hăv′ ə bär′bə kyōō′] 95/J

110

have a heart attack
    [hăv′ ə härt′ ə tăk′]   75/B
have a picnic [hăv′ ə pĭk′nĭk]   95/J
have an operation
    [hăv′ ən ŏp′ ə rā′shən]   64/A
Hawaii [hə wŏ′ē]   98/11
Head [hĕd]   60
head [hĕd]   58/11
headache [hĕd′ăk′]   62/3
headlights [hĕd′līts′]   77/2
Health Care Items [hĕlth′ kër′ ī′təmz]   65
heart [härt]   59/26
heart attack, have a
    [hăv′ ə härt′ ə tak′]   75/B
heat, no [nō′ hēt′]   32/5
heating pad [hē′tĭng păd′]   65/6
heavy [hĕv′ē]   12/4, 52/1
heel [hēl]   59/22
Height [hīt]   12/101
high [hī]   52/7
high blood pressure [hī′ blŭd′ prĕsh′ ər]   63/13
high chair [hī′ chër′]   43/9
hiking, go [gō′ hī′kĭng]   92/B
hip [hĭp]   58/7
hold [hōld]   91/I
Holidays, Celebrate the
    [sĕl′ ə brāt′ dhə hōl′ə dāz]   94–95
home, come [kŭm′ hōm′]   15/M
homesick [hōm′ sĭk′]   19/14
hood [hood]   77/4
hose [hōz]   31/11
hot [hŏt]   8/9
hot dog [hŏt′ dög′]   44/13
hot water, no [nō′ hŏt′ wŏ′tər]   32/7
hot water, bottle [hŏt′ wŏt′ ər bŏt′əl]   65/7
house, leave the [lēv′ dhə hows′]   15/J
Household Problems
    [hows′hōld′ prŏb′ləmz]   32–33
housekeeper [hows′kē′pər]   84/4
houses, build [bĭld′ how′zəz]   88/J
Houses and Surroundings
    [how′zəz ənd sə rown′dĭngz]   22
Housework [hows′würk′]   28–29
hug [hŭg]   81/G
hungry [hŭng′grē]   19/11
hurricane [hür′ə kān]   74/13
husband [hŭs′bənd]   16/9

I

ice cream [īs′ krēm′]   45/21
ice pack [īs′ păk′]   65/5

icy [īs′sē]   8/6
ID card [ī′ dē′ kärd′]   55/10
Idaho [ī′də hō′]   98/12
ignition [ĭg nĭsh′ən]   77/11
Illinois [ĭl′ə noy′]   98/13
in [ĭn]   54/6
in front of [ĭn frŭnt′əv]   54/7
inch [ĭnch]   101
Indian Ocean [ĭn′dē ən ō′shən]   96/13
Indiana [ĭn′dē ăn′ə]   98/14
Indoor Activities [ĭn′dör ăk tĭv′ə tēz]   93
infected toe [ĭn fĕk′təd tō′]   63/16
ingredients, mix [mĭks′ ĭn grē′dē ənts]   47/K
injection [ĭn jĕk′shən]   64/4
injection, give an [gĭv′ ən ĭn jĕk′shən]   67/I
Injuries [ĭn′jə rēz]   62–63
insect bite [ĭn′sĕkt bīt′]   62/11
instrument, play an
    [plā′ ən ĭn′strə mənt]   93/I
insurance card [ĭn shoor′əns kärd′]   66/4
insurance card, show
    [shō′ ĭn shoor′əns kärd′]   67/D
insurance form [ĭn shoor′əns förm′]   66/3
intercom [ĭn′tər kŏm′]   23/13
Intersection [ĭn′tər sĕk′shən]   72–73
intersection [ĭn′tər sĕk′shən]   72/6
into [ĭn′too]   79/8
Iowa [ī′ə wə]   98/15
iron [ī′ərn]   56/7, 56/C
ironing board [ī′ər nĭng börd′]   56/6

J

jacket [jăk′ət]   50/1
janitor [jăn′ə tər]   84/8
January [jăn′yoo ër′ē]   4/1
jar of coffee [jär′əv kö′fē]   37/7
jeans [jēnz]   49/4
Jewelry [joo′lə rē]   55
job, get a [gĕt′ ə jŏb′]   20/D
juice [joos]   39/20
July [joo lī]   4/7
June [joon]   4/6

K

Kansas [kăn′zəs]   98/16
Kentucky [kĕn tŭk′ē]   98/17
ketchup [kĕch′əp]   39/25
kettle [kĕt′əl]   25/3
kilogram [kĭl′ə grăm′]   101
kilometer [kĭ lŏm′ə tər]   101
kiss [kĭs]   17/C

Kitchen [kǐch′ən] 25
kitchen sink [kǐch′ən sǐngk′] 25/10
knee [nē] 59/18
knife [nīf] 42/12

L

ladder [lǎd′ər] 31/10
lamb [lǎm] 36/7
lamp [lǎmp] 24/6
large [lärj] 12/7, 53/19
laugh [lǎf] 17/B
Laundromat [lön′drə mǎt] 56
laundry, do the [dōō′ dhə lön′drē] 29/P
laundry basket [lön′drē bǎs′kət] 56/5
lawn [lön] 22/8
lawn, mow the [mō′ dhə lön′] 29/R
lawn mower [lön′ mō′ ər] 31/14
lawyer [lö′yər] 86/10
lay [lā] 87/E
leaking ceiling [lē′kǐng sē′lǐng] 32/1
leaking roof [lē′kǐng rōōf′] 32/1
learn [lürn] 15/L
leave [lēv] 81/B
leave the house [lēv′ dhə hows′] 15/J
leaves, rake the [rāk′ dhə lēvz′] 28/I
leg [lěg] 58/14
Leisure [lē′zhər] 92–93
lemons [lě′mənz] 35/7
Length [lěngkth] 101
lengthen [lěng′thən] 57/E
letter [lět′ər] 71/5
letter, mail a [māl′ ə lět′ər] 73/F
letter carrier [lět′ər kǎr′ē yər] 71/3
lettuce [lět′əs] 34/3
librarian [lī′ brěr′ē ən] 83/12
library [lī′brěr′ē] 83/13
license plate [lī′səns plāt′] 77/1
Life Events [līf′ ə věnts′] 20–21
light [līt] 52/2
light blue [līt′ blōō′] 9/16
limes [līmz] 35/8
line [līn] 70/5
lip [lǐp] 60/10
Liquid Measure [lǐk′wǐd mězh′ər] 101
listen [lǐs′ən] 3/F
listen to music [lǐs′ən tə myōō′zǐk] 93/L
liter [lēt′ər] 101
little [lǐt′əl] 12/8
Living Room [lǐv′ǐng rōōm′] 24
load [lōd] 56/A
loaf of bread [lōf′ əv brěd′] 37/5

lobby [lǒb′ē] 23/9
lobster [lǒb′stər] 36/11
lock, broken [brō′kən lǒk′] 32/8
locksmith [lǒk′ smǐth′] 84/3
long [löng] 53/13
long hair [löng′ hěr′] 13/11
look at the clothes [lōōk′ ǎt dhə klōz′] 73/H
look at the screen [lōōk′ ǎt dhə skrēn′] 3/H
look at the windows
  [lōōk′ ǎt dhə wǐn′dōz] 73/H
loose [lōōs] 53/16
Louisiana [lōō wē′ zē ǎn′ə] 98/18
love, fall in [föl′ ǐn lŭv′] 21/F
low [lō] 52/8
luggage [lŭg′əj] 80/3
lung [lŭng] 59/25

M

mail, deliver [də lǐv′ər māl′] 89/R
mail a letter [māl′ ə lět′ər] 73/F
mailbox [māl′ bǒks′] 71/4
mailboxes [māl′bǒks′əz] 23/11
Maine [mān] 98/19
maintenance man [mān′tə nənts mān′] 85/17
make a phone call [māk′ ə fōn′ köl′] 73/C
make a toast [māk′ ə tōst′] 94/B
make the bed [māk′ dhə běd′] 28/A
mall [möl] 69/19
man [mǎn] 11/5
Maps [mǎps] 96–99
March [märch] 4/3
margarine [mär′jə rǐn] 38/7
market, fruit and vegetable
  [frōōt′ ǎnd vej′tə bəl mär′ kət] 83/18
married, get [get′ mǎr′ēd] 21/G
Maryland [měr′ə lənd] 98/20
mashed potatoes [mǎsht′ pə tā′tōz] 45/19
Massachusetts [mǎs′ə chōō′sǐts] 98/21
May [mā] 4/5
mayonnaise [mā′ ə nāz′] 39/26
Meal, Cooking a [kōōk′ǐng ə mēl′] 46–47
measure [měhz′ər] 87/G
Measures [měhz′ərz] 101
measuring tape [měhz′ə rǐng tāp′] 101
Meat [mēt] 36
meat, cut [kŭt′ mēt′] 88/E
meat, ground [grownd′ mēt′] 36/3
mechanic [mə kǎn′ ǐk] 82/3
Medical Office [měd′ ə kəl ö′ fǐs] 66–67
medicine [měd′ ə sən] 64/1
medicine, take [tāk′ měd′ ə sən] 64/D

medicine cabinet [mĕd′ə sən kăb′ə nət] 27/9
medicine chest [mĕd′ə sən chĕst′] 27/9
medicine dropper [mĕd′ə sən drŏp′ər] 64/6
medium [mē′dē əm] 53/18
meet [mēt] 81/E
Memorial Day [mə mör′ē əl dā′] 94
menu [mĕn′yōō] 43/8
messenger [mĕs′ən jər] 86/5
meter [mē′tər] 101
mice [mīs] 33/14
Michigan [mĭsh′ə gən] 98/22
microwave oven [mī′krə wāv′ ŭv′ən] 25/1
middle-aged [mĭd′əl ājd′] 13/23
midnight [mĭd′nīt′] 7/3
mile [mīl] 101
milk [mĭlk] 38/1
milk, carton of [kär′tən əv mĭlk′] 37/1
milk, drink [drĭnk′ mĭlk′] 17/H
milk, pour [pör′ mĭlk′] 47/J
milligram [mĭl′ə grăm′] 101
milliliter [mĭl′ə lē′tər] 101
Minnesota [mĭn′ə sō′tə] 98/23
mirror [mĭr′ər] 27/8
Mississippi [mĭs′ə sĭp′ē] 98/24
Missouri [mĭ zŏŏr′ē] 98/25
mittens [mĭt′ənz] 50/12
mixed ingredients [mĭks′ ĭn grē′dē ənts] 47/K
Monday [mŭn′dā] 5/2
Money [mŭn′ē] 10
money order [mŭn′ē ör′dər] 71/12
Montana [mŏn tăn′ə] 98/26
Months [mŭnths] 4
moon [mōōn] 6/6
mop [mŏp] 30/1
mop the floor [mŏp′ dhə flör′] 29/O
morning [mör′nĭng] 6/1
mother [mŭdh′ər] 16/3
motorcycle [mō′tər sī′kəl] 76/5
mouth [mowth] 60/6
move [mōōv] 21/J
mover [mōō′vər] 84/9
movie theater [mōō′vē thē′ə tər] 69/18
movies, go to the
   [gō′ tə dhə mōō′vēz] 93/J
mow the lawn [mō′ dhə lön′] 29/R
muffin [mŭf′ən] 44/5
mugging [mŭg′ĭng] 74/9
mushrooms [mŭsh′rōōmz] 34/14
music, listen to [lĭs′ən tə myōō′sĭk] 93/L
mustache [mŭs′tăsh] 13/10
mustard [mŭs′tərd] 39/24

N

nail [nāl] 31/15
name, print [prĭnt′ nām′] 67/B
name, sign [sīn′ nām′] 67/C
nap, take a [tāk′ ə năp′] 91/G
napkin [năp′kĭn] 42/10
narrow [nă′rō] 52/9
Natural disasters
   [năch′ə rəl dĭz ăs′tərz] 74–75
Nebraska [nə brăs′kə] 98/27
neck [nĕk] 58/2
necklace [nĕk′lĭs] 55/4
needle [nē′dəl] 57/1
nephew [nĕf′yōō] 16/15
nervous [nür′vəs] 18/4
Nevada [nə văd′ə] 98/28
new [nōō] 52/3
New Hampshire [nōōz′ hămp′shər] 98/29
New Jersey [nōō′ jür′zē] 98/30
New Mexico [nōō′ mĕk′sə kō] 98/31
New Year's Eve [nōō′ yïrz ēv′] 94
New York [nōō′ yörk′] 98/32
newspapers, sell [sĕl′ nōōz′pā pərz] 88/I
newsstand [nōōz′ stănd′] 72/7
next to [nĕkst′ tōō] 54/3
nickel [nĭk′əl] 10/5
niece [nēs] 16/14
night [nīt] 6/4
night table [nīt′ tā′bəl] 26/14
nightgown [nīt′ gown′] 51/9
nipple [nĭp′əl] 90/5
no heat [nō′ hēt′] 32/5
no hot water [nō′ hŏt′ wö′tər] 32/7
no smoking section
   [nō′ smō′kĭng sek′shən] 43/11
noodles [nōō′dəlz] 39/17
noon [nōōn] 7/2
north [nörth] 97/15
North America [nörth′ ə mĕr′ə kə] 96/4
North Atlantic Ocean
   [nörth′ ăt lăn′tĭk ō′shən] 96/11
North Carolina [nörth′ kăr′ə lī′nə] 99/33
North Dakota [nörth′ də kō′tə] 99/34
North Pacific Ocean
   [nörth′ pə sĭf′ĭk ō′shən] 96/9
northeast [nörth ēst′] 97/19
northwest [nörth wĕst′] 97/20
nose [nōz] 60/9
nose, bloody [blŭd′ē nōz′] 63/17
notebook [nōt′bŏŏk′] 2/12
notebook, open a [ō′pən ə nōt′bŏŏk′] 3/J

November [nō vĕm′bər]   4/11
nurse [nürs]   66/7
nuts [nŭts]   35/14

O

Occupations [ŏk′ yə pā′shənz]   82–86
Oceans [ō′shənz]   96
October [ŏk tō′bər]   4/10
office [ö′fĭs]   83/16
office building [ö′fĭs bĭl′dĭng]   69/17
Ohio [ō hī′ō]   99/35
oil [oyl]   38/14
ointment [oynt′mənt]   64/3
Oklahoma [ō klə hō′mə]   99/36
old [ōld]   13/24, 52/4
on [ŏn]   54/5
On the road [ŏn dhə rōd′]   78–79
onion [ŭn′yən]   34/12
onions, slice [slīs′ ŭn′yənz]   46/D
open a card [ō′pən ə kärd′]   17/J
open a notebook [ō′pən ə nōt′bŏŏk′]   3/J
operation, have an
    [hăv′ ən ŏp′ə rā′shən]   64/A
orange [ör′ĭnj]   9/12
oranges [ör′ĭnj əz]   35/4
Oregon [ör′ə gən]   99/37
ounces [own′səz]   101
out of [owt′əv]   79/9
Outdoor Activities [owt′ dör′ ăk tĭv′ə tēz]   92
outlet [owt′lət]   30/12
oven [ŭv′ən]   25/7
over [ō′vər]   78/1
oversee [ō′vər sī′]   87/D

P

Pacific Ocean, North
    [nörth′ pə sĭf′ĭk ō′shən]   96/9
Pacific Ocean, South
    [sowth′ pə sĭf′ĭk ō′shən]   96/10
pacifier [păs′ə fī′ər]   90/3
pack [păk]   41/H
package [păk′ĭj]   71/2
package of cookies
    [păk′ĭj əv kŏŏk′ēz]   37/4
packages, deliver [də lĭv′ər păk′ĭj əz]   89/T
Packaging [păk′ĭj ĭng]   37
packer [păk′ər]   40/12
Pains [pānz]   62–63
paint [pānt]   87/K
paint Easter eggs [pānt′ ē′stər ĕgz′]   94/E
painter [pān′tər]   84/6

pajamas [pə jŏm′əz]   51/10
pan [păn]   25/5
pancakes [păn′kāks′]   44/7
panties [păn′tēz]   51/4
pants [pănts]   48/7
pantyhose [păn′tē hōz′]   51/5
paper [pā′pər]   2/9
paper towels [pā′pər tow′əlz]   30/10
parade, watch a [wŏch′ ə pə rād′]   94/H
paramedic [păr′ə mĕd′ĭk]   74/6
parents [păr′ənts]   16/11
park [pärk]   68/7
parking garage [pär′kĭng gə röj′]   69/15
parking lot [pär′kĭng lŏt′]   69/21
parking meter [pär′kĭng mē′tər]   72/8
Party, Birthday [bürth′dā pär′tē]   17
passenger [păs′ĭn jər]   80/1
pasta [pŏs′tə]   39/17
patient [pā′shənt]   66/5
patient, examine the
    [ĭg zăm′ĭn dhə pā′shənt]   67/F
patient, weigh the
    [wā′ dhə pā′shənt]   67/G
patio [pă′tē ō′]   22/11
pay for [pā′ för]   41/C
peaches [pē′chəz]   35/10
pears [përz]   35/5
peas [pēz]   34/15
pedestrian [pə dĕs′trē ən]   72/2
peel potatoes [pēl′pə tā′tōz]   46/A
pen [pĕn]   2/10
pencil [pĕn′səl]   2/11
Pennsylvania [pĕn′səl vān′yə]   99/38
penny [pĕn′ē]   10/4
People [pē′pəl]   11
People, Describing [dəs krī′bĭng pē′pəl]   12–13
pepper [pĕp′ər]   39/23
pepper, bell [bĕl′ pĕp′ər]   34/9
pepper shaker [pĕp′ər shā′kər]   42/9
peppers, chop [chŏp′ pĕp′ərz]   46/E
pharmacist [fär′mə sĭst]   82/1
phone [fōn]   24/7
phone call, make a [māk′ ə fōn′ köl′]   73/C
photographer [fə tŏg′rə fər]   86/6
pick out [pĭk′ owt′]   41/D
pick up [pĭk′ ŭp′]   91/K
pick up the room [pĭk′ ŭp′ dhə rŏŏm′]   28/B
picnic, have a [hăv′ ə pĭk′nĭk]   95/J
picture, take a [tāk′ ə pĭk′chər]   17/G
pie, apple [ăp′əl pī′]   45/22
pillow [pĭl′ō]   26/8

pillowcase [pĭl′ō kās′]		26/9
pills [pĭlz]		64/2
pilot [pī′lət]		80/8
pink [pĭnk]		9/15
pint [pīnt]		101
pipes, fix [fĭks′ pīps′]		88/C
pipes, repair [rə për′ pīps′]		88/C
pizza [pēt′sə]		45/16
place mat [plās′ măt′]		42/3
plane [plān]		76/8
plant a tree [plănt′ ə trē′]		29/Q
plants, water the [wö′tər dhə plănts′]		28/H
plate [plāt]		42/5
play [plā]		91/C
play an instrument		
[plā′ ən ĭn′strə mənt]		93/I
play baseball [plā′ bās′böl′]		92/G
play basketball [plā′ băs′kət böl′]		92/E
play football [plā′ fōōt′böl′]		92/D
play soccer [plā′ sŏk′ər]		92/F
play tennis [plā′ tĕn′əs]		92/C
playpen [plā′pən′]		90/9
pliers [plī′ərz]		31/I
plumber [plŭm′ər]		84/1
plums [plŭmz]		35/9
point (to) [poynt′ tōō]		3/B
poison, swallow [swŏl′ō poy′zən]		75/D
police officer [pə lēs′ öf′ə sər]		74/8
police station [pə lēs′ stā′shən]		68/5
pools, take care of [tāk′ kër′ əv pōōlz′]		89/M
pop [pŏp]		39/19
porch [pörch]		22/3
pork [pörk]		36/4
pork chop [pörk′chŏp′]		45/18
Post Office [pōst′ öf′ĭs]		71
post office [pōst′ öf′ĭs]		68/4
postal clerk [pōs′təl klürk′]		71/1
postal worker [pōs′təl wür′kər]		71/1
postcard [pōst′ kärd′]		71/11
pot [pŏt]		25/2
potato [pə tā′tō]		34/11
potato, baked [bākt′ pə tā′tō]		45/17
potatoes, mashed [măsht′ pə tā′tōz]		45/19
potatoes, peel [pēl′ pə tā′tōz]		46/A
pound [pownd]		101
pour [pör]		87/F
pour milk [pör′ mĭlk′]		47/J
Prepared Foods [prə përd′ fōōdz′]		44–45
Prepositions [prĕp′ə zĭ′shənz]		54, 78–79
prescription [prĭ skrĭp′shən]		66/10
prescription, write a		
[rīt′ ə prĭ skrĭp′shən]		67/J
present, give a [gĭv′ ə prĕz′ənt]		17/A
print name [prĭnt′ nām′]		67/B
public telephone [pŭb′lĭk tĕl′ə fōn]		72/4
pumpkin, carve out a		
[kärv′ owt′ ə pŭmp′kən]		95/L
purple [pür′pəl]		9/13
purse [pürs]		55/5
push [pŏŏsh]		41/A
put in [pŏŏt′ in′]		41/E, 56/A, 87/B

Q

quart [kwört]		101
quarter [kwör′tər]		10/7
quarter cup, a [ə kwör′tər kŭp′]		101

R

rag [răg]		30/5
raincoat [rān′kōt′]		50/8
raining [′rā′nĭng]		8/1
raise . . . hand [rāz′ . . . hănd′]		3/K
rake [rāk]		31/12
rake the leaves [rāk′ dhə lēvz′]		28/I
range [rānj]		25/6
rash [răsh]		62/10
rattle [răt′əl]		90/11
razor [rā′zər]		61/8
read [rēd]		3/E
receipt [rə sēt′]		10/12
receptionist [rə sĕp′shə nəst]		66/2
red [rĕd]		9/6
red hair [rĕd′ hër′]		13/18
refrigerator [rə frĭj′e rā′tər]		25/16
refrigerator not working		
[rə frĭj′ə rā tər nŏt′ wür′kĭng]		33/12
repair appliances [rə për′ ə plī′əns əz]		88/A
repair cars [rə për′ kärz′]		88/B
repair pipes [rə për′ pīps′]		88/C
repair TVs [rə për′ tē vēz′]		88/A
reporter [rə pör′tər]		86/7
rest, get [gĕt′ rĕst′]		64/B
Restaurant [rĕs′tə rənt]		43
retire [rĭ tīr′]		20/E
return address [rə türn′ ə drĕs′]		71/7
Rhode Island [rōd′ ī′lənd]		99/39
rice [rīs]		39/15
ring [rĭng]		55/1
roaches [rō′chəz]		33/13
robbery [rŏb′ər ē]		74/7
rock [rŏk]		91/H
roll of toilet paper [rōl′ əv toy′lət pā′pər]		37/9

roof [rōof]   22/2
roof, leaking [lē′kĭng rōof]   32/1
room, pick up the [pĭk′ ŭp′ dhə rōom′]   28/B
room, straighten up the
   [strā′tən ŭp′ dhə rōom′]   28/B
Routines, Daily [dā′lē rōo tēnz′]   14–15
rubber gloves [rŭb′ər gluvz′]   30/7
rug [rŭg]   24/10
rug, vacuum the [văk′yōom dhə rŭg′]   28/D
ruler [rōo′lər]   101
run [rŭn]   91/E
running, go [gō′ rŭn′ĭng]   93/N

S

sad [săd]   18/3
salad [săl′əd]   45/14
salesperson [sālz′pür′sən]   86/11
salt [sölt]   39/22
salt shaker [sölt′ shā′kər]   42/9
sandals [săn′dəlz]   49/5
sandwich [sănd′wĭch]   44/10
sanitation worker
   [săn′ə tā′shən wür′kər]   83/19
Saturday [săt′ər dā]   5/7
saucer [sö′sər]   42/8
sausage [sö′sĭj]   44/2
saw [sö]   31/5
scale [skāl]   40/7
scared [skërd]   18/6
scarf [skärf]   50/10
school [skōol]   68/1
school, start [stärt′ skōol′]   20/B
scissors [sĭz′ərz]   57/3
scrambled eggs [skrăm′bəld ĕgz′]   44/1
scrape [skrāp]   87/J
screen, look at the
   [lōok′ ăt dhə skrēn′]   3/H
screw [skrōo]   31/16
screwdriver [skrōo′drī′vər]   31/3
scrub brush [skrŭb′ brŭsh′]   30/8
Seafood [sē′fōod′]   36
seamstress [sēm′strĭs]   57/6
Seasons [sē′zənz]   4
seat belt [sēt′bĕlt′]   77/14
secretary [sĕc′rə tër′ē]   86/1
security check [sə kyōor′ə tē chĕk′]   80/4
security guard [sə kyōor′ə tē gärd′]   70/3
sell clothes [sĕl′ klōz′]   88/G
sell newspapers [sĕl′ nōoz′pā pərz]   88/I
sell vegetables [sĕl′ vĕj′tə bəlz]   88/H
send cards [sĕnd′ kärdz′]   95/R

September [sĕp tĕm′bər]   4/9
service station [sür′vĭs stā′shən]   82/5
sew [sō]   57/A
sewing machine [sō′ĭng mə shēn′]   57/7
sewing machine operator
   [sō′ĭng mə shēn′ ŏp′ə rā′tər]   85/22
shake hands [shāk′ hăndz′]   81/F
shampoo [shăm pōo′]   61/5
Shapes [shāpz]   9
shave [shāv]   14/G
shaving cream [shā′vĭng krēm′]   61/7
sheets [shēts]   26/12
sheets, change the [chānj′ dhə shēts′]   29/L
shelf [shĕlf]   40/1
ship [shĭp]   76/10
shirt [shürt]   48/4
shoe [shōo]   48/8
Shoe store [shōo′ stör′]   54
shoes, athletic [ăth lē′tĭk shōoz′]   49/8
shopping basket [shŏp′ĭng băs′kət]   40/3
shopping cart [shŏp′ĭng kärt′]   40/4
short [shört]   12/3, 53/14
short hair [shört′ hër′]   13/12
shorten [shört′ən]   57/F
shorts [shörts]   49/9
shorts, boxer [bŏk′sər shörts′]   51/2
shot [shŏt]   64/4
shot, give a [gĭv′ ə shŏt′]   67/I
shoulder [shōl′dər]   58/3
shovel [shŭv′əl]   31/13
show insurance card
   [shō′ ĭn shōor′əns kärd′]   67/D
shower [show′ər]   27/1
shower, take a [tāk′ ə show′ər]   14/C
shower curtain [show′ər kür′tən]   27/2
shrimp [shrĭmp]   36/12
sick, get [gĕt′ sĭk′]   21/K
sidewalk [sĭd′wök′]   72/9
sign name [sīn′ nām′]   67/C
signature [sĭg′nə chər]   70/9
silverware [sĭl′vər wër′]   42/2
sing [sĭng]   17/E
singer [sĭng′ər]   86/14
sink [sĭngk]   27/7
sister [sĭs′tər]   16/4
sit [sĭt]   3/M
Size [sīz]   12
skiing, go [gō′ skē′ĭng]   92/H
skillet [skĭl′ət]   25/5
skinny [skĭn′ē]   12/6
skirt [skürt]   48/3

sleep, go to [gō′ tə slēp′]	15/P	
Sleepwear [slēp′wër′]	51	
slice onions [slīs′ŭn′yənz]	46/D	
slippers [slĭp′ərz]	51/12	
slot [slŏt]	56/4	
small [smöl]	12/8,53/17	
smile [smīl]	17/D	
smoke [smōk]	74/1	
smoking sections [smō′kĭng sek′shən]	43/10	
sneakers [snē′kərz]	49/8	
sneeze [snēz]	63/A	
snowing [snō′ĭng]	8/2	
soap, bar of [bär′ əv sōp′]	37/11	
soccer, play [plā′ sŏk′ər]	92/F	
socks [sŏks]	51/8	
soda [sō′də]	39/19	
soda, bottle of [bŏt′əl əv sō′də]	37/3	
sofa [sō′fə]	24/11	
soldier [sōl′jər]	85/21	
Solid Weights [sŏl′əd wāts′]	101	
son [sŭn]	16/12	
sore throat [sör′ thrōt′]	62/12	
soup [sōōp]	39/18	
soup, can of [kăn′ əv sōōp′]	37/8	
south [sowth]	97/16	
South America [sowth′ ə mër′ə kə]	96/5	
South Atlantic Ocean [sowth′ ăt lăn′tĭk ō′shən]	96/12	
South Carolina [sowth′ kăr′ə lī′nə]	99/40	
South Dakota [sowth′ də kō′tə]	99/41	
South Pacific Ocean [sowth′ pə sĭf′ĭk ō′shən]	96/10	
southeast [sowth ēst′]	97/21	
southwest [sowth wĕst′]	97/22	
spaghetti [spə gĕt′ē]	39/17, 45/15	
spinach [spĭn′əch]	34/4	
sponge [spŭnj]	30/9	
Spoon [spōōn]	42/13	
sports [spörts]	92	
spray [sprā]	64/7	
spring [sprĭng]	4/14	
square [skwër]	9/3	
stairs [stërz]	23/12	
stairway [stër′wā′]	23/12	
stamp [stămp]	71/8	
stand [stănd]	3/N	
stars [stärz]	6/7	
start school [stärt′skōōl′]	20/B	
steak [stāk′]	36/2	
steam vegetables [stēm′ vĕj′tə bəlz]	47/I	
steering wheel [stĭr′ĭng wēl′]	77/10	
stepladder [stĕp′ lăd′ ər]	31/10	
steps [stĕps]	23/6	
steps, broken [brō′kən stĕps′]	33/9	
stereo [stĕr′ē ō]	24/13	
stereo system [stĕr′ē ō sĭs′təm]	24/13	
stir onions and peppers [stŭr′ŭn′yənz ənd pĕp′ərz]	46/G	
stitches, get [gĕt′stĭch′əz]	64/C	
stockings [stŏk′ĭngz]	51/6	
stomach [stŭm′ək]	59/27	
stomachache [stŭm′ək āk′]	62/5	
stop [stŏp]	73/D	
stopped-up toilet [stŏpt′ ŭp′ toy′lət]	32/6	
stove [stōv]	25/6	
straight hair [strāt′ hër′]	13/14	
straighten up the room [strā′tən ŭp′ dhə rōōm′]	28/B	
strawberries [strö′bër′ēz]	35/11	
street, cross the [krös′ dhə strēt′]	73/E	
string beans [strĭng′ bēnz′]	34/7	
stroller [strō′lər]	90/2	
student [stōō′dənt]	2/5	
study [stŭd′ē]	15/L	
subway [sŭb′wā′]	76/7	
sugar [shŏŏg′ər]	38/3	
suit [sōōt]	48/9	
suitcase [sōōt′kās′]	80/3	
summer [sŭm′ər]	4/15	
sun [sŭn]	6/5	
Sunday [sŭn′dā]	5/1	
sunglasses [sŭn′glăs′əz]	49/3	
sunny [sŭn′ē]	8/4	
superintendent [sōō′pər ĭn tĕn′dənt]	84/10	
Supermarket [sōō′pər mär′kət]	40–41	
supermarket [sōō′pər mär′kət]	68/11	
surprised [sər prīzd′]	19/8	
swallow poison [swŏl′ō poy′zən]	75/D	
sweater [swĕt′ər]	50/3	
sweatshirt [swĕt′shürt′]	50/5	
sweep the floor [swēp′ dhə flör′]	29/M	
swimming, go [gō′ swĭm′ĭng]	93/M	
swimsuit [swĭm′sōōt′]	49/1	
swimtrunks [swĭm′trŭnks′]	49/2	
swollen ankle [swō′lən ăng′kəl]	63/15	
syrup [sĭr′əp]	44/8	

T

table [tā′bəl]	42/1	
table, coffee [kö′fē tā′bəl]	24/9	
table, end [ĕnd′ tā′bəl]	24/8	
table, night [nīt′ tā′bəl]	26/14	

Table Setting [tā′bəl sĕt′ĭng]	42
tablespoon [tā′bəl spōōn′]	101
Tailor [tā′lər]	57
tailor [tā′lər]	57/8
take a nap [tāk′ ə năp′]	91/G
take a picture [tāk′ ə pĭk′chər]	17/G
take a shower [tāk′ ə show′ər]	14/C
take care of children [tāk′ kër′ əv chĭld′rən]	89/L
take care of grounds [tāk′ kër′ əv growndz′]	89/N
take care of pools [tāk′ kër′ əv pōōlz′]	89/M
take medicine [tāk′ mĕd′ə sən]	64/D
take out [tāk′ owt′]	41/F, 56/B, 87/A
take out the garbage [tāk′ owt′ dhə gär′bĭj]	28/J
take . . . temperature [tāk′ . . . tĕm′pər ə chər]	67/H
talk [tök]	3/L
tall [töl]	12/1
tape measure [tāp′ mĕzh′ ər]	31/7
taxi [tăk′sē]	76/6
taxi driver [tăk′sē drī′vər]	84/12
taxicab [tăk′sē kăb′]	76/6
tea [tē]	38/12
teacher [tē′chər]	2/4
teakettle [tē′kĕt′ əl]	25/3
teaspoon [tē′spōōn′]	101
teenager [tēn′ā′jər]	11/7
telephone [tĕl′ə fōn′]	24/7
telephone, public [pŭb′lĭk tĕ′lə fōn′]	72/4
television [tĕl′ə vĭzh′ ən]	24/14
teller [tĕl′ər]	70/1
temperature [tĕm′pər ə chər]	8/8
Tennessee [tĕn′ə sē′]	99/42
tennis, play [plā′ tĕn′əs]	92/C
Texas [tĕk′səs]	99/43
Thanksgiving [thăngks gĭv′ ĭng]	95
theft [thĕft]	74/7
thermometer [thər mŏm′ə tər]	65/3
thigh [thī]	59/16
thin [thĭn]	12/6
third of a cup, a [ə thürd′ əv ə kŭp′]	101
thirsty [thürs′tē]	19/12
thread [thrĕd]	57/2
through [thrōō]	78/4
thumb [thŭm]	58/9
Thursday [thürz′dā]	5/5
ticket [tĭk′ət]	80/2
tickets, collect [kə lĕkt′ tĭk′əts]	89/W
tie [tī]	48/5
tight [tīt]	53/15
Time [tīm]	4–7
Times of Day [tīmz′ əv dā′]	6
tire [tīr]	77/8
tired [tīrd]	19/10
to [tōō]	78/2
toast [tōst]	44/4
toast, make a [māk′ ə tōst′]	94/B
toaster [tōs′tər]	25/13
today [tə dā′]	5/12
toe [tō]	59/23
toe, infected [ĭn fĕk′təd tō′]	63/16
toilet [toy′lət]	27/12
toilet, stopped-up [stŏpt′ ŭp′ toy′lət]	32/6
toilet paper [toy′lət pā′pər]	27/13
toilet paper, roll of [rōl′ əv toy′lət pā′pər]	37/9
Toiletries [toy′lə trēz]	61
tomato [tə mā′tō]	34/8
tomorrow [tə mŏr′ ō]	5/13
tongue [tŭng]	60/12
toolbox [tōōl′ bŏks′]	31/9
Tools [tōōlz]	31
tooth [tōōth]	60/11
toothache [tōōth′ āk′]	62/6
toothbrush [tōōth′ brŭsh′]	61/4
toothpaste [tōōth′ pāst′]	61/3
toothpaste, tube of [tōōb′ əv tōōth′ pāst′]	37/12
tornado [tör nā′dō]	74/12
toward [törd]	78/2
towel [tow′əl]	27/11
toy [toy]	90/7
traffic light [trăf′ək līt′]	72/1
train [trān]	76/9
train conductor [trān′ kən dŭk′tər]	85/23
train station [trān′ stā′shən]	69/14
Transportation [trăns′pər tā′shən]	76
trash can [trăsh′ kăn′]	25/11
Treatments [trēt′mənts]	64
tree, decorate the [dĕk′ə rāt dhə trē′]	95/T
tree, plant a [plănt′ ə trē′]	29/Q
triangle [trī′ăng′gəl]	9/2
trick-or-treating, go [gō′ trĭk′ər trē′tĭng]	95/N
truck [trŭk]	76/3
truck, drive a [drīv′ ə trŭk′]	89/Q
truck driver [trŭk′ drīv′ ər]	85/19
trunk [trŭngk]	77/6
try on [trī′ ŏn′]	57/C
T-shirt [tē′shürt′]	49/7

tube of toothpaste
    [tōōb′ əv tōōth′ pāst′]   37/12
Tuesday [tōōz′ dā]   5/3
turkey [tür′ kē]   36/9
turn [türn]   73/J
TV [tē vē′]   24/14
TV, watch [wŏch′ tē vē′]   93/K
TVs, fix [fĭks′ tē vēz′]   88/A
TVs, repair [rə për′ tē vēz′]   88/A
typist [tī′ pəst]   86/2

U

umbrella [ŭm brĕl′ ə]   50/9
uncle [üng′ kəl]   16/6
under [ŭn′ dər]   54/9
underpants [ŭn′ dər pănts′]   51/3
undershirt [ŭn′ dər shürt′]   51/1
Underwear [ŭn′ dər wër′]   51
uniform [yōō′ nə förm′]   48/11
United States of America, the
    [dhə yōō nī′ təd stāts′
    əv ə mër′ ə kə]   98–99
unload [ŭn lōd′]   56/B
up [ŭp]   79/6
Utah [yōō′ tö]   99/44

V

vacuum cleaner [văk′ yōōm klē′ nər]   30/4
vacuum the rug [văk′ yōōm dhə rŭg′]   28/D
valentines, give [gĭv′ văl′ ən tīnz′]   94/C
Valentine's Day [văl′ ən tīnz′ dā′]   94
van [văn]   76/4
vegetable market, fruit and
    [frōōt′ ănd vēj′ tə bəl mär′ kət]   83/18
Vegetables [vej′ tə bəlz]   34
vegetables, sell [sĕl′ vej′ tə bəlz]   88/H
vegetables, steam [stēm′ vej′ tə bəlz]   47/I
Vermont [vür mŏnt′]   99/45
vest [vĕst]   50/2
Virginia [vər jĭn′ yə]   99/46
visit a cemetery [vĭz′ ət ə sĕm′ ə tër′ē]   94/I

W

waffles [wŏf′ əlz]   44/6
waist [wāst]   58/6
wait [wāt]   67/E
wait for the bus [wāt′ för dhə bŭs′]   73/K
waiter [wā′ tər]   43/6
waiting room [wā′ tĭng rōōm′]   66/1
waitress [wā′ trəs]   43/7
wake up [wāk′ ŭp′]   14/A

walk [wök]   73/I
walker [wök′ ər]   65/9
wall [wöl]   24/2
wall, cracked [krăkt′ wöl′]   32/2
wallet [wŏl′ ət]   55/9
warm [wörm]   8/10
warm-up suit [wörm′ ŭp sōōt′]   49/10
wash the dishes [wŏsh dhə dĭsh′ əz]   28/F
wash the windows [wŏsh dhə wĭn′ dōz]   29/N
washcloth [wŏsh′ klŏth′]   61/6
washer [wŏsh′ ər]   56/1
wash . . . face [wŏsh′ . . . fās′]   14/E
washing machine [wŏsh′ ĭng mə shēn′]   56/1
Washington [wŏsh′ ĭng tən]   99/47
wastebasket [wāst′ băs′ kət]   27/6
wastebasket, empty the
    [em′ tē dhə wāst′ băs′ kət]   29/K
watch [wŏch]   55/6
watch a parade [wŏch′ ə pə rād′]   94/H
watch fireworks [wŏch′ fīr′ würks′]   95/K
watch TV [wŏch′ tē vē′]   93/K
water [wŏ′ tər]   43/4
water, boil [boyl′ wŏ′ tər]   46/B
water the plants [wŏ′ tər dhə plănts′]   28/H
watermelons [wŏ′ tər mĕl′ ənz]   35/13
wave [wāv]   81/C
wave a flag [wāv′ ə flăg′]   94/G
wave good-bye [wāv′ gōōd bī′]   81/C
wavy hair [wāv′ ē hër′]   13/15
wear a costume [wër′ ə kŏs′ tyōōm]   95/M
Weather [wĕdh′ ər]   8
Wednesday [wĕnz′ dā]   5/4
week [wēk]   5/15
weigh [wā]   41/G
weigh the patient [wā′ dhə pā′ shənt]   67/G
Weight [wāt]   12
Weights [wāts]   101
west [wĕst]   97/18
West Virginia [wĕst′ vər jĭn′ yə]   99/48
wet [wĕt]   53/11
wheelchair [wēl′ chër′]   65/10
white [wīt]   9/5
wide [wīd]   52/10
wife [wīf]   16/10
window [wĭn′ dō]   22/5
window, broken [brō′ kən wĭn′ dō]   32/3
window, close the [klōz′ dhə wĭn′ dō]   3/I
window, drive-thru [drīv′ thrōō wĭn′ dō]   70/2
windows, look at the
    [lōōk′ ăt dhə wĭn′ dōz]   73/H
windows, wash the [wŏsh dhə wĭn′ dōz]   29/N

119

windshield [wĭnd′shēld′]   77/5
windy [wĭn′dē]   8/3
winter [wĭn′tər]   4/13
Wisconsin [wĭs kŏn′sən]   99/49
withdrawal slip [wĭdh dröl′ slĭp′]   70/10
woman [wŏŏm′ən]   11/4
word processor [würd′ prŏ′sĕs ər]   86/2
work [würk]   15/K, 88−89
work at the computer
   [würk′ ăt dhə kəm pyōō′tər]   3/G
Workplaces [würk′plā′səz]   82−83
World, the [dhə würld′]   96−97
worried [wür′ēd]   19/9
wrench [rĕnch]   31/2
wrist [rĭst]   58/10
write [rīt]   3/A
write a prescription
   [rīt′ ə prə skrĭp′shən]   67/J
Wyoming [wī ō′mĭng]   99/50

X
X ray [eks′rā′]   66/9

Y
yard [yärd]   101
yardstick [yärd′stĭk′]   101
year [yïr]   5/16
yellow [yĕl′ō]   9/8
yesterday [yĕs′tər dā]   5/11
yogurt [yō′gərt]   38/8
yogurt, container of
   [kən tā′nər əv yō′gərt]   37/2
young [yŭng]   13/22

Z
zip code [zĭp′kōd′]   71/10
zipper [zĭp′ər]   57/5